P9-CST-142

Country
FURNITURE

A WALLACE-HOMESTEAD PRICE GUIDE

Country FURNITURE

ELLEN M. PLANTE

Wallace-Homestead Book Company
Radnor, Pennsylvania

For Ted

Copyright © 1993 by Ellen M. Plante
All rights reserved

Published in Radnor, Pennsylvania 19089, by Wallace-Homestead Book Company,
a division of Chilton Book Company

No part of this book may be reproduced, transmitted or stored
in any form or by any means, electronic or mechanical,
without prior written permission from the publisher

Photography by Ted Plante unless otherwise noted.

Designed by Anthony Jacobson

Pie safe shown on the cover from the collection of Kathryn Wesley Hotchkiss

Manufactured in the United States of America

Library of Congress Cataloging-in-Publication Data
Plante, Ellen M.
    Country furniture / Ellen M. Plante ; photos by Ted
Plante.
        p.   cm.
    Includes bibliographical references and index.
    ISBN 0-87069-640-8
    1. Country furniture—United States—History—19th century—
Catalogs.   2. Country furniture—United States—History—20th
century—Catalogs.   I. Title.
NK2407.P63   1993
749.213′075—dc20   92-32289
                                                              CIP

1 2 3 4 5 6 7 8 9 0   2 1 0 9 8 7 6 5 4 3

Contents

Preface

As we move toward the new century, *country* and *country furniture* have taken on new meaning. We are no longer confined to viewing a limited range of objects as being of *country* origin. During the 1970s and even the early 1980s, country furniture was thought to be primitive, crude pieces constructed in straightforward fashion; today we know better.

This book will take you on a tour of today's country furniture market. Along with the primitive cupboards, benches, stools, and other pieces recognized as country a decade ago, we've learned that this category must also include many of the products of the machine age and developments of the early twentieth century. The American country style didn't cease to exist with the dawn of the Industrial Revolution; instead, it experienced a rebirth that added new dimensions to its classic appeal.

The photographs on the following pages were, for the most part, taken at large outdoor antiques shows with dealer representation from across the country and Canada. Photos of auction pieces were provided courtesy of *AntiqueWeek*. As with any price guide, the collector must be aware that supply and demand, the area of the country, trends, and other factors will directly influence pricing. The prices quoted within are *asking* prices for items pictured unless otherwise noted.

Acknowledgments

This book would not have been possible without the kind interest and cooperation of the many dealers who allowed us to photograph their country furniture pieces and assorted country collectibles. They took time during busy antiques shows to offer assistance, answer questions and even move furniture for us. To the following, we extend a very sincere thank-you: AAA & Antiques, Geneva, New York; Anona's Antiques, Roulette, Pennsylvania; Antiques American, Chagrin Falls, Ohio; Dennis and Valerie Bakoledis, Rhinebeck, New York; J.E. Barker Antiques, St. Catharines, Ontario, Canada; Tim Bennett, Westfield, New York; Bruce Bishop/Larches Antiques, Waterloo, New York; Cora Bissell, Kendall, New York; Bittersweet Antiques, Gaylordsville, Connecticut; Blue Goose Antiques, Fulton, New York; Blue Stores Antiques & Auction Service, Livingston, New York; Bonnie Montgomery, Jefferson, New York; Brown Durby Antiques, Fall River, Massachusetts; Burnham's Hidden Treasures, Newark, New York; Butez Antiques, Johnstown, New York; Caroline Byfield Antiques, Kitchener, Ontario, Canada; Joan Caldwell, Pittsford, New York; 1780 Cape Antiques, Laconia, New Hampshire; Carousel Antiques, at the Antique Barn, Leway, New York; Casey's Antiques, Germantown, New York; Sheila Cassin, Fairport, New York; Chelsea Hill Antiques, Hampton, Connecticut; Clarke Antiques, Corning, New York; The Closetful, Clinton, New York; Cobweb Corner Antiques, Sharon, Pennsylvania; Copper Indian Antiques, Rome, New York; Country Antiquing, Canandaigua, New York; The Country Barn Shop, Wilson, New York; Country Corner Antiques, Petrolia, Ontario, Canada; Country House Antiques, Hawkestone, Ontario, Canada; Country Lady Antiques, Saratoga Springs, New York; Creekside Acres Antiques, Alden, New York; Will Crell, Virginia Beach, Virginia; Linda Dawson, Rochester, New York; DeRitter Antiques, Hinsdale, New York; John B. Dodge, Bedford, Massachusetts; Dordick & Husted Antiques, Woodstock, New York; Edgewood Antiques, Rochester, New York; Edward L. Faria, Middleboro, Massachusetts; Farm Full Antiques, Verona, New York; George Francis Antiques & Collectibles, South Egremont, Massachusetts; Granny's This & That, Gloversville, New York; Robert Grefford-Au Bon Dieux Temps Antiquites, Lanoraie, Province of Quebec, Canada; Wendy B. Hamilton Antiques, Oakville, Ontario, Canada; George Hemming, Pittsford, New York; Heritage Guest House B&B and Antique Shop, Dushore, Pennsylvania; Hilltop Antiques, Skowhegan, Maine; Hurst's Collectables, Ridgeway, Ontario, Canada; Holly Cobbles, Fairport, New York; Hourglass Art & Antiques Gallery, Albany, New York; Andy Howe, Lobo, Ontario, Canada; Humby's Sundries, Rochester, New York; Iron Eagle Antiques, Chenango Forks, New York; Harry Jebbett, Cortland, New York; Judy's Antique Co-op, Franklinville, New York; Keefer's Antiques, Bristol, New York; William Lary Antiques, Peterborough, New Hampshire; March Hare Antiques, Plainville, Connecticut; James and Karen McKee,

Orillia, Ontario, Canada; Memories Antiques & Collectibles, Fayetteville, New York; Barbara Minear Antiques & Santa Dolls, Warsaw, Indiana; Mockingbird Antiques & Collectibles, Northboro, Massachusetts; Monkton Mill Antiques, Monkton, Maryland; Helen and Tony Morrison Antiques & Collectibles, Waterford, Connecticut; My Favorite Things Antiques, Preston, Connecticut; Nana's Attic, Duxbury, Massachusetts; Old Friend Antiques & Collectables, Rochester, New York; Old Roxbury Antiques, Brockport, New York; Patti's Antiques & Treasures, Indian Orchard, Massachusetts; Peg's Choice Antiques, East Aurora, New York; Pink Swan Antiques, Holyoke, Massachusetts; Don and Norine Plato, St. Catharines, Ontario, Canada; Puddle Duck Antiques, Plaistow, New Hampshire; Mimi Pyne Antiques, Lewiston, New York; Pieces of the Past Antiques, Canandaigua, New York; Rader Antiques, Holcomb, New York; Reflections Antiques, Williamson, New York; Retired Early Antiques, Telford, Pennsylvania; Ridge Antiques, Spencerport, New York; Riverview Antiques, W. Napanee, Ontario, Canada; Sheila Rose, Rochester, New York; Ruth's Antiques, Clarence, New York; Bob Scott and Peter Bisback, Bruce County, Western Ontario, Canada; Settlers Effects Antiques, Oshawa, Ontario, Canada; Simcoe Reflections, Barrie, Ontario, Canada; Nathan Smith House Antiques, Cornish, New Hampshire; Snow Country Antiques & Collectibles, Derry, New Hampshire; Judy and Leo Srodawa—1880 Antiques, Honeoye Falls, New York; Murray E. Stewart Antiques, Lunenburg, Nova Scotia, Canada; Surprise Shop Antiques, Annapolis, Maryland; Susquehanna Antique Center, Granville, New York; T's Antiques, Bouckville, New York; The Little Store Antiques, Great Barrington, Massachusetts; Thru the Years, New Hampton, New York; Vi and Si's Antiques, Ltd., Clarence, New York; Wagon Wheel Antique Mall, Oxford, Maine; H.G. Well's Antiques & Collectibles, Batavia, New York; The Wicker Porch Antiques, Marion, Massachusetts; Wilson's Antiques, Mansfield, Pennsylvania; and Melinda and Laszlo Zongor, Bedford, Pennsylvania.

I would like to extend special thanks to Tom Hoepf, editor of the Central Edition of *AntiqueWeek* for sending additional photos of auction pieces for illustration. I'd like to thank the following auctioneers and auction houses for the use of their photos: Mike Clum, Inc., Rushville, Ohio; Delbert Cox Auctioneers, Hamilton, Ohio; Tim and Glen Speck, Auctioneers, Perrysburg, Ohio; Paul Cuskaden and Associates, St. Paul, Illinois; Tom Prater and Steve Pinciaro, Auctioneers, Unity, Ohio; Dragoo Auction Company, Gaston, Indiana; Highway #99 Auctions, Columbia, Tennessee; Lawson Brothers Auctioneers, Danville, Indiana; Riverbent Antiques, West Virginia; Joe Penn Auctioneer, Shelbyville, Kentucky; Joy Luke Auctioneer, Bloomington, Illinois; Hutchinson Auction Inc., Albany, Ohio; AppleTree Auction Center, Newark, Ohio; Page Auction, Crossville, Tennessee; and Jack Woods Auction, New Carlisle, Ohio.

I would like to thank Tony Cubello of Covenant Studios, Lewiston, New York, and James Shannahan of JBS Photo Service, North Tonawanda, New York, for all the time and hard work invested in preparing our black-and-white photographs.

Finally, special thanks to my manuscript editor, Tim Scott, who is always encouraging and a pleasure to work with, and thank you to Acquisitions Editor Susan Clarey and Editorial Consultant Harry Rinker at Wallace Homestead for giving me the opportunity to write this book on country furniture.

Harry Rinker and his staff at Rinker Enterprises were also instrumental in obtaining additional photos to use in illustrating this book, and for that I am very appreciative.

SECTION I
An Introduction to Country Furniture

The Origins of Country Furniture

American country furniture includes those utilitarian, often simplistic forms created to fill a specific need. Initially, function was of primary importance in constructing country furniture pieces, and while they may not sport numerous carved designs or regal embellishments, they are nevertheless appreciated and coveted for their plain lines, individuality and historic significance.

During the eighteenth and early nineteenth centuries, country furniture pieces were handcrafted at home with whatever materials were readily available or turned out by village craftsmen who had varying degrees of skill. By the second half of the nineteenth century, country furniture also was being machine-made at numerous young factories.

Rural living found the farmer, lum-

Jelly cupboard with original blue-green paint, four shelves inside, 34″ wide × 15½″ deep × 60″ tall, **$1250.**

Shoe-foot blanket chest with older green paint, 40″ wide × 14″ tall, **$500.**

Hutch table, a circa 1900 replica of an eighteenth-century table, pine top with an oak base, 54″ wide × 37½″ deep × 29½″ tall, **$650.**

Hutch table pictured previously, with top lifted to provide seating and storage.

berman, blacksmith and others with little time to spare (other than winter) or money to devote to furniture making. They crafted tables, benches, cupboards and beds as quickly as possible with little or no ornamentation except for the occasional coat of paint used to give the piece unity in appearance. (See Section II for information on painted country furniture.)

The country furniture pieces made by village craftsmen or traveling carpenters often incorporated features from furniture styles popular in the larger towns and urban areas. Some of these craftsmen had limited or no formal training but produced sturdy furniture pieces to meet the needs of the farmers and villagers, while sometimes incorporating just a hint of the English or European influence found in formal furniture. The styles they borrowed from may already have faded from production in the city; it was often years before

Rocker, circa 1850, traces of old red paint, a Canadian country piece found for sale in Massachusetts, 17½″ wide × 36″ tall, **$150.**

Pine open hanging cupboard with decorative trim and old brown paint, French-Canadian piece, 32″ wide × 10″ deep × 38″ tall, **$270.**

French-Canadian half-moon table with three legs, 37″ wide × 18″ deep × 28″ tall, **$950.**

a style's influence reached the rural areas of the country. When it did, it was sometimes combined with the elements of another style or modified (scaled-down) to appeal to the conservative nature of the farmer.

As the machine age slowly took hold in the early 1800s, some country furniture pieces, such as the popular Hitchcock chair, were at least partially machine-made. When the Industrial Revolution dawned during the second half of the nineteenth century, increasing numbers of country furniture pieces were factory-produced. Attractive, painted cottage furniture is an excellent example of a popular line of furnishings that was factory-made from the 1860s on, and could be bought inexpensively to furnish vacation cottages (hence the name "cottage furniture") and smaller homes. By the late 1800s everything from kitchen cupboards and pie safes to chairs, beds and tables were being machine-made as furniture factories expanded production lines.

Ethnic Styles and Blends in Country Furniture

American country furniture exhibits a diverse range of cultural influences. As immigrants settled in different regions of the country, their ethnic background was often expressed through furniture style, construction or decoration.

To fulfill dreams of a better life in America, they came from England, Germany, France, Ireland, Scotland, Italy, Scandinavia and numerous other regions. Most immigrants arrived in America with little more than personal belongings stored safely in the family blanket chest, and they relied on their own skills and years of cultural tradition to fashion furniture pieces once they settled in the new land. For example, when Scandinavians began arriving in America in the 1820s, they crafted home furnishings from native woods found throughout Wisconsin and Minnesota. Following age-old customs, they embellished their furniture with carvings and decorative painting. An especially popular painted finish known as rosemaling was achieved by decorating large pieces such as chests, cupboards and benches with brightly colored flowers and leaves.

As French and French-Canadian settlers made their homes in Louisiana and along the Mississippi River, they crafted beautiful armoires (wardrobes) from local hardwoods such as cherry and walnut. These armoires were turned out in French tradition, combining scalloped skirts and delicate cabriole legs to give these pieces a distinctive and easily recognized style.

The Spanish brought to the American Southwest unique furniture designs characterized by massive size and bold lines. A combination of Spanish influence and Native American customs yielded pieces decorated with carvings and carved incised lines that were often highlighted with colorful paints. The Spanish influence is clearly evident in the free-standing kitchen cupboards produced throughout the late 1800s and early 1900s in many regions of the Southwest. These cupboards were often painted to imitate geometric tiles and/or vivid textile designs, and they echo a cultural relationship with color and form.

Probably the best known ethnic or religious influences on furniture design originated with the Shakers and the Pennsylvania Dutch.

The Shakers

The Shaker sect (formally known as The United Society of Believers in Christ's Second Appearing) was

Mt. Lebanon Shaker slat-back chair with unusually large seat, 21″ wide × 18″ deep × 34″ tall, **$725.**

founded in 1774 by Ann Lee of Manchester, England. She and eight others came to America and settled the first Shaker community at Watervliet near Albany, New York, in 1776. Until her death in 1784, Mother Ann Lee and other Shaker representatives conducted mission tours that resulted in the organization of Shaker communities in Connecticut, Massachusetts, New Hampshire, New York, Maine, Ohio, Kentucky and Indiana. The Shaker community at New Lebanon, New York (the name was changed to Mount Lebanon in the 1860s), was the main ministry and the largest community in the East.

Shakerism embodied simplicity, purity, harmony and order. These fundamental principles yielded a furniture style that was simple and plain—and quite beautiful.

The craftsmen and cabinetmakers in the various Shaker communities crafted similar furniture pieces to fur-

Excellent Shaker style two-piece secretary with original red wash, blind-front cupboard doors over three small drawers, base has fold-out lid above two large drawers, circa 1820, 83″ tall × 43″ wide, sold at auction for **$11,000**. Photo courtesy of *AntiqueWeek.*

One-drawer Shaker dry sink with old red paint, sold at auction for **$2700**. Photo courtesy of *AntiqueWeek.*

nish the large dwellings that housed up to 100 believers. For example, they made very long tables and benches and extra-large cupboards for storage. Pine was most often used, but Shaker furniture also employed maple, chestnut, birch, cherry and butternut in settlements located in Ohio, Kentucky and Indiana.

The Shaker cabinetmaker developed a distinctive style, and his work is recognized and identified today by his design and construction methods of exposed dovetail joints, an obvious lack of moldings and decorative hardware, very narrow cupboard doors, combination pieces, the incorporation of small drawers on stands and tables, and the use of simple wooden pegs as drawer pulls. Pieces were either left plain and varnished or painted red, green or yellow. Early chairs had a splint, cane or leather seat while later examples were made with rush seats or colorful tape seats.

By 1874 the Shaker craftsmen at Mount Lebanon, New York, were turning out chairs, benches and other small items that were sold to the public through illustrated catalogs. Soon other Shaker communities followed in the commercial production of goods (mainly chairs, rockers and benches) and these pieces continued to be made and sold through the 1930s. The sale of Shaker chairs and rockers reached an all-time high during the late nineteenth century after a display of chairs won an award for "Strength, Sprightliness and Modest Beauty" at the 1876 Philadelphia Centennial. The Shakers peddled these goods (along with seeds, brooms

Shaker stepstool with original green paint, classic arch construction, molded front legs, 13" wide × 21" tall, **$2800.**

Shaker "apple sorting" chair with one slat-back, tape seat of light and dark blue, 18" wide × 12" deep × 26" tall, **$850.**

Shaker footstool, tape (cream and maroon) over original splint, 12" wide × 9" deep × 9" tall, **$275.**

and brushes and colorfully painted oval wooden boxes in assorted sizes) to country stores close to their settlements.

One of the Mount Lebanon catalogs issued during the 1870s offered three types of chairs for sale, including slat-back, web-back and upholstered chairs. Customers could order chairs with or without rockers and arms. The Shaker rockers were available in eight different sizes, with #0, the smallest, being a child-size chair. Rockers were usually stained with a dark finish. Tape seats could be ordered from among 14 different colors: black, brown, gold, scarlet, drab, orange, maroon, pomegranate, three different shades of green, and three variations of blue.

The Shaker communities thrived from 1800 to 1860, and their membership grew from 1000 to 6000 followers. After the Civil War the population of the Shaker sect began to dwindle, with many leaving to join the outside world. By the turn of the century, only about 1000 members remained.

The Pennsylvania Dutch

During the late seventeenth century, the first group of Pennsylvania Dutch immigrants came to America to escape hunger, poor living conditions and religious persecution in Germany.

Ohio Amish two-piece step-back cupboard, chestnut and walnut, blind-front, cutout pie shelf with three drawers underneath, in excellent, original condition, 89″ tall × 62″ wide, sold at auction for **$900**. Photo courtesy of *AntiqueWeek*.

Some of these people, who settled in the southeastern region of Pennsylvania, were also from France, Sweden, Denmark and Switzerland, but they collectively are known as "Pennsylvania Deutsch" (or Dutch), which means Germans.

The majority of these early Pennsylvania settlers were farmers and belonged to one of several religious groups, including the Amish, Moravians, Lutherans, Reformed, and Mennonites.

Some of the early furniture pieces crafted by these people were plain and utilitarian, but by the early 1800s the Pennsylvania Dutch love of color and decoration brought with them from Europe became evident in their furniture designs. Their noteworthy dower chests, plank chairs and schranks (large cupboards), often were embellished with a brightly painted finish, carved design, stenciling or hand-painting.

Dower chests usually were made of pine or tulip poplar, with or without bottom drawers, and typically had bracket feet. They often were painted red, blue or brown. A dower chest, made for a young girl to store belongings for her future marriage, often was decorated with her name and the date the chest was made or given. Stenciled or hand-painted flowers, birds, fruits, stars, and other designs adorned these dower chests, making them a beautiful combination of color and design. Sometimes a dower chest was decorated with spatter-painting, graining, sponging, or marbling to imitate the grain of a wood or add a swirled or other decorative touch.

Pennsylvania two-piece corner cupboard in original salmon and mustard paint with finger and sponged decorations, 12-pane (6 × 6) upper doors, pie shelf, two drawers, circa 1820, 82″ tall, sold at auction for **$6000.** Photo courtesy of *AntiqueWeek.*

Germanic cupboard, circa 1885, paint has been restored (red with traces of blue), 48″ wide × 18″ deep × 82″ tall, **$1400.**

Teakwood cupboard found in Blue Ball, Pennsylvania, old blue and red painted designs, 45″ wide × 18″ deep × 64″ tall, **$2600.**

Plank chairs are another Germanic furniture piece the Pennsylvania Dutch brought to America. A simple stool-like piece with splayed legs, the plank chair also had a decorative curved back often enhanced with carvings. Plank chairs were usually made of black walnut, cherry or maple.

The schrank was used to store clothing. It often was made with drawers at the bottom and usually two (but sometimes only one) doors. Two-door examples were made with shelves on one side for storing folded clothes or linens and the other side was used to hang clothing. Elaborate schranks were usually very large (eight feet tall), made of black walnut or cherry, and decorated with carved designs and moldings. Like late-eighteenth- and early nineteenth-century dower chests, schranks are a rare find today and cost thousands of dollars. Many have survived the years but are housed in small museums or are part of private collections. Often a simple, sometimes smaller schrank was made of pine and then painted and decorated with tulips, hearts, birds, and geometric designs that the Pennsylvania Dutch loved. A painted example would also be a rare find. Today, softwood, painted schranks are being imported from Germany.

By the mid-1800s the strong Germanic influence in furniture design and vibrant decorations slowly disappeared as the Industrial Revolution dawned and other people moved into the area. A small number of Pennsylvania Dutch settlers chose to leave, moving west to Ohio, south to North Carolina and north to Canada.

The Industrial Revolution

While early country furniture was created to fill a specific need, that need began to change over the years as architectural development, the domestic sciences and the Industrial Revolution brought about bigger houses, new inventions and machine-made products. By the mid-nineteenth century the influence of the growing Industrial Revolution resulted in many country furniture pieces being partially machine-made. Machines were used for stamping, molding, embossing and plating; the circular saw was in use; and furniture-making shops used a modified assembly line for production, utilizing both the master craftsman and the worker with limited skills.

In the 1842 publication *Cottage Residences* by Andrew Jackson Downing, gaily painted cottage furniture and spool-turned beds and tables were illustrated. These affordable furnishings were geared toward the working class and therefore became a big success. Machine-made goods created new possibilities in home decoration. Even in rural areas there was a keen interest in the latest styles or inventions albeit on a smaller scale.

As inexpensive machine-made furniture began to appeal to the growing number of middle-class Americans, the country was expanding through the railroads that linked the vast expanses together. Today we realize the country furniture category also includes the many factory-made oak pieces that could be ordered through the mail-order catalogs and shipped to even the most remote areas of the country.

We must also consider and include

Lady's oak rocker with pressed-back design, 17" wide × 16" deep × 40" tall, **$140.**

Oak rocker, circa 1910, with original pressed-back seat, excellent condition, 20" wide × 40" tall, **$285.**

Oak highchair, 17″ wide × 21″ deep × 38″ tall, **$210.**

Wicker rocker with cane seat, painted black, 24″ wide × 20″ deep × 38″ tall, **$165.**

the rustic twig chairs, tables, benches, and other pieces that were made from the late 1800s through the 1940s and were initially created to satisfy the Victorians' desire to return to nature while in the midst of their newly industrialized society.

Finally, no discussion of American country furniture would be complete without recognizing the simple wicker chairs, rockers, tables, planters, and other furniture forms that graced front porches and furnished sun rooms from the turn-of-the-century through the 1930s.

SECTION II
Country Furniture Know-How

Country Furniture Defined for the 1990s

"Country" today not only refers to a type of furniture, but also to a style that has evolved into an American way of life. We embrace tradition and both respect and appreciate the beauty and simplicity found in the furnishings, textiles, crafts and day-to-day tools of past generations. In our search for an escape or reprieve from the fast-paced world and sleek state-of-the-art technology, Americans have collectively designated "home" a safe haven where we can surround ourselves with objects that give us comfort, pleasure and a sense of belonging to the past.

In *The Country Home Book*, (Simon and Schuster, New York 1989), author Miranda Innes writes ". . . there is a look—almost an attitude—that evokes the country at its best. It has to do with celebrating what you have, looking at your home and your possessions with a fresh eye and exploiting their particular charms. It is a tradition that is strong on ingenuity. . . ."

The evolution of country style into a way of life has resulted in an eclectic potpourri of country furnishings that span the 1800s right through the 1940s.

Country style draws color from the earth and sun; nature takes center stage in the materials used for furnishings; and America's melting pot of cultural diversity gives us the variety found in country for the 1990s.

As a result, there is no single look to country; rather, there are several. For example, country furnishings today reflect the understated beauty found in

Doughbox, pine and chestnut, circa 1820, lid original with new braces, 48″ wide × 21½″ deep × 29″ tall, **$395.**

Sack-back armchair, black over old blue paint, 22″ wide × 15″ deep × 34″ tall, **$950.**

Pine hanging cupboard with ten drawers, 18″ wide × 36″ tall, **$85.**

Tiger maple grandfather clock with broken arch, oval burl inlaid medallion in door and base, circa 1810, 94″ tall, sold at auction for **$4100.** Photo courtesy of *AntiqueWeek.*

18

the more formal pieces turned out by skilled high-country craftsmen; the appealing simplicity of homemade utilitarian goods; the American Southwest style influenced by the Indians, Spaniards and Anglo-Americans; and the spirituality which contributed to the design of the Shaker movement. Country furnishings also exhibit the charm of the English cottage; the vibrant colors and textures of the French countryside; the ingenuity of the nineteenth-century machine age; and the remnants of the Victorian back-to-nature movement.

American country furniture is a unique element of a culturally rich heritage which will continue to be the focus of a style and way of life for years to come.

Identifying Style and Construction Methods

Furniture styles have changed and gone through periods of popularity since the time of the Pilgrims, often with one style blending into another. Each distinct "period" influenced the on-going development of country furniture in that skilled craftsmen would take design elements from a particular style (or even a combination of styles) and incorporate them into their furnishings. The end result was usually a more subtle expression of style or period influence; a scaled-down piece that would appeal to the tastes of the rural population. Chronologically we classify furniture styles accordingly:

Early Colonial/Pilgrim (1630–1700)
The furniture of this period was large, massive and reminiscent of medieval days. Oak and pine were commonly used woods.

William and Mary (1690–1730)
This particular style was named after the king and queen of England who reigned from 1689–1694. This style is characterized by many decorations, curved lines and carvings of Baroque influence. The gateleg table and rush seats were popular during this period.

Queen Anne (1725–1760)
This delicate style is named after the queen who ruled England from 1702–1714. The Queen Anne period popularized the cabriole leg and the use of mahogany in furniture making.

Chippendale (1750–1795)
This graceful furniture style was named after a London cabinetmaker, Thomas Chippendale, and introduced the claw and ball foot, incorporated carved decorations, and popularized slat-back side chairs.

Federal (1780–1840)
This style includes geometric lines and classic decorations. This period introduced the Martha Washington chair, an upholstered easy chair that was especially popular in New England and is recognized by its low seat, high back and open arm rests.

Empire (1815–1840)
Named in honor of Emperor Napoleon (who ruled 1804–1814), this style is characterized by elegant decorations, gilt stenciling, paw feet and the use of dark woods in furniture construction. The sleigh bed became popular during

this period, and many beautiful country pieces with grain painting were inspired by the Empire style.

Shaker (1790–1900)
Named after the religious sect that produced simple, utilitarian furniture pieces, Shaker furniture is today an important component of the American country furniture style. (For further information on Shaker style, refer to the Introduction.)

Revival (1840–1900)
During this time period, Gothic (1840–1880), Rococo (1840–1870) and Renaissance (1850–1880) Revival styles captured the attention of the Victorians and brought architectural embellishments, bold designs, and nature's influence to an era noted for swift changes and growing industrialization.

Eastlake (1870–1890)
Named after arts reformer Charles Eastlake, this modernistic machine-made furniture is highlighted by incised linear and geometric decorations.

Art Nouveau (1895–1910)
Made popular by the "back to nature" movement (in response to growing industrialism and machine-made goods), Art Nouveau brought wispy curves and flowers to the furnishings and decorations of the late Victorian era. Rustic twig furniture filled the remote "camps" where Victorians fled to escape the changing world.

Mission/Arts and Crafts (1900–1925)
This style is characterized by plain, utilitarian design. The sudden change in wicker furnishings—from ornate to plain—was a direct result of the Arts and Crafts movement and new technology that created machine-manufactured wicker. Mission oak furnishings filled the pages of the popular mail-order catalogs.

Country (1800–1940)
While handcrafted furniture pieces have been built since the Early Colonial/Pilgrim period, the heyday of country furniture really began early in the nineteenth century. The country furniture style is characterized by simple and plain handcrafted, utilitarian pieces; pieces that echo European influence, ethnic flair or religious simplicity and beauty; early products of the machine age that furnished vacation cottages or rural homes, rustic twig furnishings, simple front porch wicker, and those unembellished and sturdy factory-produced goods that found their way into most middle American homes.

Throughout the centuries the formal furniture designs often overlapped one another. The skilled craftsmen that

Child's pine rocker, 13″ wide × 30″ tall, **$70.**

Unusual "gunstock" chairs, circa 1870, made in England, 18″ wide × 32″ tall, **$60 each.**

Pennsylvania cherry corner cupboard, 16 panes (8 × 8), with nicely shaped skirt, circa 1800, 82″ tall, sold at auction for **$3100.** Photo courtesy of *AntiqueWeek.*

created high-style country furniture in cities such as Philadelphia, New York, and Boston were keenly aware of this and for the most part followed the dictates of any given style.

In contrast, some less-sophisticated rural craftsmen did not feel compelled to follow a strict code of design. They freely mixed styles and took from a style those design aspects they found appealing or useful to create a simple version of more elaborate furniture; a piece that would add a touch of style to the country or rural home and at the same time maintain hard-working practicality.

Homemade country furniture pieces were crafted to meet a specific need and were therefore often devoid of ornamentation. Their simplicity gives them subtle elegance, and pieces with a painted finish have a special time-honored beauty.

Numerous books, magazines, and magazine articles devoted to the country style have been written and published during these past few decades and continue to be published today.

In *Early American Furniture* (Alfred A. Knopf, New York, 1970), author John T. Kirk tells us, "in primitive furniture there seems to be a greater lightness of touch, almost a sense of humor; it is more intriguing, more eccentric, more patterned; and it often depends upon its surface quality to make it delightful."

In 1980, when Mary Emmerling wrote *American Country: A Style and Source Book*, (New York: Clarkson N. Potter, Inc.), she told us, "houses decorated with painted furniture, quilts, and baskets, tables set with stoneware and pewter . . . we call this style of decorating, and of living, American Country."

Since these words were written, the country style has evolved and expanded to include the various examples of furniture, folk art, crafts, and household necessities that span the nineteenth and

New England country Sheraton washstand, circa 1820, dove-tailed construction, maple and pine, 17″ wide × 13″ deep × 36½″ tall, **$295.**

Eighteenth-century hutch table with original gray paint, sold at auction for **$1575.** Photo courtesy of *AntiqueWeek.*

early twentieth centuries. No longer restricted to the "primitive" look that predominated during the 1970s and early 1980s, today's country furniture "style" is at the same time American and yet international in scope, formal, primitive, Victorian, rustic and exemplifies the ingenuity that was the focus of the nineteenth century machine age.

Country style can be equally at home in a metropolitan high-rise, where a tramp art mirror and rustic twig chair take center stage and add to eclectic design; in a farmhouse where "fancy" is kept to a minimum and sturdy furnishings such as an old jelly cupboard filled with vintage collectibles and a long pine table outfit the kitchen; in a suburban rancher where a painted corner cupboard and heirloom Oriental rug bring the family room warmth and color; in a Queen Anne Victorian where factory-made oak furniture fills every room and pays tribute to the changing world; in a cozy cottage where scaled-down furniture, colorful cushions and small collectibles take you back in time; and in the apartment where furnishings are most important in making a personal statement, and even a single piece (such as a beautiful French armoire, a painted chest or vintage wicker chair) can say "country style."

Being able to recognize and identify the construction methods and hardware used in country furniture will help pinpoint age and alert a buyer to reproductions and fakes.

Knowing the difference between a butt joint and a dovetailed joint, for example, will reveal the strength of a piece and aid the collector in a thorough examination to make sure there is consistency in construction.

By studying the overall appearance of a piece, we can also note the type of wood or woods used in construction; decide if the piece is proportionally cor-

A set of six plank-seat chairs, inscribed "1839 Utica," painted and stenciled, 13½" wide × 32½" tall, **$1800 for the set.**

A six-board pine blanket box, 37″ wide × 18″ deep × 17½″ tall, **$125.**

rect; check for tool marks (which will also aid in determining age); and lastly, consider the patina (the outward appearance of the piece, which is conditioned by exposure to air, light, scrubbings, polishings and everyday wear and tear over a number of years).

Country furniture was constructed of either hardwoods or softwoods or a combination of both. Hardwoods are deciduous trees (meaning trees that shed their leaves in winter) and include oak and oak look-alikes such as elm and ash, walnut, cherry, mahogany, chestnut, maple and birch. Softwoods are conifers or evergreens such as pine, spruce, cedar, fir and hemlock.

Construction tells us a great deal about a piece, and examination will reveal if it is authentically handmade, partially machine-made, or the product of a factory.

When looking at country furniture construction, the type of *joint* used in putting the piece together is of major importance. Early construction employed several different joints.

Butt Joint

This is a somewhat crude and less than desirable method of construction in which one board is "butted" up against the other and then nailed. Over time these joints loosen and can separate.

Mortise and Tenon Joint

Used in the construction of furniture by the ancient Greeks, the mortise and tenon is considered the strongest, most durable method of joining wood together. This is a common method of constructing chairs, tables and case pieces, and while different types of mortise and tenon joints were employed, basically all involved a tongue (or tenon) that was placed into a corresponding hole (or mortise) in another piece of wood and then reinforced with pegs and later, glue.

Dovetail Joints

Used since the late 1600s (but invented by the Egyptians), dovetail joints were a popular method of construction in which a "dovetail"-shaped piece of wood is cut to fit into a corresponding

24

On the left, factory-made step-back kitchen cupboard with glass-front doors, **$800–$1000**; and on the right, step-back cupboard with blind-front doors and pie shelf, **$1000–$1500**. Photo courtesy of *AntiqueWeek*.

Baker's table, pine, unusual design, made in Pennsylvania, 31″ wide × 24½″ deep × 28″ tall, **$150.**

slot. Early dovetail joints employed only one or two large dovetails while other hand-cut examples employed more. By 1860 machine-made dovetail joints were made, resulting in more numerous dovetails with uniformity in size. Dovetail joints were open or concealed and most often found in drawer construction.

This is a very strong and durable method of construction. Collectors should keep in mind that multiple dovetails of uniform size indicate a later, machine-made piece of furniture.

In examining furniture construction, a collector should also look for tool marks. For example, a scribe mark or scribe line is a mark or narrow groove made with a sharp tool that outlines how pieces will be joined together. Although dovetail joints could be machine-made after the 1860s, many pieces continued to be constructed by hand. Hence, scribe marks can be found on some dovetailed pieces made through the 1880s.

Furniture made before 1850 may have smoothing plane marks, which are repetitive ridges on drawer bottoms or sides made by a plane or scraper.

Saw marks are also very revealing in determining the age of a piece. Until 1850, saw marks were straight. These "up and down" saw marks were created by early saws driven by windmills and waterwheels. After 1850 the circular saw, which was powered by steam engines, was widely used in furniture construction and left curved saw marks. (Check drawer bottoms for such marks.)

Hardware is also to be considered when examining the construction of a piece of furniture. For example, nails can reveal or help pinpoint the age of a piece. Up until 1814, handwrought nails were sharply pointed and had round or rectangular heads. By 1815 machinery had been developed that could turn out nails that had square heads and were tapered to a blunt end. These machine-cut nails were widely used until 1890, at which time round-headed wire nails came into use.

Hand-cut wood screws, with their uneven threads, were used until 1815 and then machine-made screws were introduced. These machine-made examples (used until 1845) had even screw threads, a well-centered slot in the head, and blunt ends. Pointed ends were introduced during the second half of the nineteenth century.

Regarding handles, the 1800s saw simple country pieces given wooden knobs, wooden peg pulls, white porcelain knobs, or drawer pulls of a carved or molded fruit design. Metal (often brass) rectangular pulls were used at the turn of the twentieth century.

Keyhole escutcheons on country pieces were usually made of wood, iron or brass.

Buying in Today's Market

Buying country furniture (as well as other antiques and collectibles) today requires us to be knowledgeable collectors. Gone are the days of finding treasures in the roadside trash or picking up pristine pieces for a next-to-nothing cost. The supply of certain country furniture pieces (painted furniture, for example) is too small and the demand too great. Unfortunately, reproductions have entered the market.

Collectors must educate themselves. There are numerous books and magazines available for antiques and collectibles enthusiasts. It is equally important to visit and explore museums, antiques shops and shows, auctions, flea markets, and other venues and closely inspect the furniture pieces you find there.

Pay attention to special exhibits that feature reproductions and fakes. These are increasingly being included at larger antiques shows in an ongoing ef-

Primitive Pennsylvania pine cupboard from Bucks County, 24″ wide × 25″ deep × 54″ tall, **$525.**

Pine sideboard with original graining, 48″ wide × 17″ deep × 44″ tall, **$795.**

Round one-drawer workstand, circa 1860, old red paint, 20″ wide × 29″ tall, **$105.**

fort to alert and educate collectors and dealers alike. Unmarked reproductions, intended to fool the public, can and do turn up anywhere. While efforts are made to monitor the merchandise at many antiques shows, reproductions have been found in shops, auctions, flea markets, and other venues. (See Hints at the end of each furniture section to learn how to avoid reproductions).

While it is important to understand the concept of style and be able to recognize construction methods, we must also know how to examine a piece of furniture so that we will not be fooled by fakes, rebuilt pieces, married pieces, and of course reproductions.

Take time to evaluate the appearance of the piece. Is it proportionally correct? (Consider, too, how it will look in your home.) What is its condition? Are there obvious repairs or replacement parts? Does the piece have the worn spots you'd expect to find from

years of use, such as scuffing and bare wood on the rung on a chair? Is the patina consistent—in other words, has the entire piece aged as a whole?

Open drawers or cupboard doors and check the construction methods. Look for tool marks on the sides and bottoms of drawers and examine the hardware. Are there nail holes where they don't seem to belong? Over time, old nails seem to sink down into the wood. Do the nails look too new? Check the backing of the piece. Old cupboards were constructed with wide boards for backing and were not originally painted.

Ask questions of the dealer/seller. Do they have knowledge of the history of the piece? Have they made or are they aware of any repairs? (Repairs do not have to be a negative aspect if they are done carefully. Accurate restoration is often needed to bring a piece back to life.)

If you make a purchase, ask the dealer to write on your receipt that the piece is as represented and/or that the finish is authentic.

Early one-drawer pine stand made in Maine, old brown paint over blue, 24″ wide × 20″ deep × 32″ tall, **$195.**

Note: Many painted country pieces have more than one coat of paint, and while the top coat may not be the original coat of paint, it can be authentically old. For example, a circa 1870 pie safe originally painted mustard, then painted blue twenty or thirty years later, does not wear an original finish but has an authentically old painted finish. (Refer to Section III for more information on painted country furniture.)

Knowing how to examine country furniture for style, construction methods, age and authenticity can be enhanced by keeping some key dates in mind.

- Wooden pins were used before 1850
- Circular saw marks appeared after 1850
- The majority of machine-made dovetails were seen after 1890
- Scribe marks on drawers for dovetails can be found on pieces made through the 1880s
- Blown glass with wavy lines and bubbles was used before 1850
- Pressed glass knobs or drawer pulls came into use after 1825
- Machine-cut threads on screws were prevalent after 1830

Country furniture can be expensive. Take time to search for just the right piece and buy the best you can afford. Most collectors will agree that the "hunt" is an important part of the pleasure they derive from an interest in antiques and collectibles, and it can often take a great deal of time to find just the right piece. Patience is an absolute necessity when investing your time and hard-earned money in antique furniture, but keep in mind that hesitation in making a purchase may lead later to regret. When you find a piece you've been

Oak youth chair with attractive pressed-back design, 14″ wide × 14″ deep × 40″ tall, **$160.**

searching for, or you realize the luck you've had in discovering a rare or unusual piece, that's the time to buy.

What Does Today's Market Offer a Collector?

Since the country furniture category for the 1990s has expanded to include items from the early twentieth century, today's country furniture market offers a collector a wide range of diversity. Nineteenth-century America gave us both handcrafted and factory-made furniture pieces that have become a part of the country style of living. While an early 1800s Shaker chair may be impossible to find, and a blue painted step-back cupboard scarce, there are still many fine handcrafted

Dark or "antique" oak pressed-back chair with cane seat, 17" wide × 16" deep × 36" tall, **$65.**

Golden oak pressed-back rocker with cane seat, 17" wide × 17" deep × 38" tall, **$165.**

country furniture pieces available. There is also a good supply of mail-order oak and front-porch wicker, and more and more collectors are taking note of the appealing rustic twig pieces that were both handcrafted and factory-produced through the 1940s.

Where to Find Country Furniture Today

Shopping for country furniture can be an exciting adventure. There are antiques shops and shows; estate sales; auctions; and seasonal, monthly or weekly flea markets to attend. In addition, don't overlook the classified advertisements in the local paper or swap sheet. Often a private individual is an

excellent source for one piece or an entire collection.

On rare occasion a smart buyer can still find a great deal at a house or yard sale. Auctions, too, can provide an opportunity for some excellent buys, but you must know the value of what you're looking for and how much you are willing to spend; most important, inspect the piece carefully and thoroughly. Local newspapers usually list upcoming auctions, as do weekly and monthly trade publications for antiques and collectibles enthusiasts.

The past decade has seen an explosion in the number of large flea markets and antiques shows held on a regular basis. Large seasonal antiques shows and flea markets like those held in

Lady's bench, painted black with upholstered seat, 20″ wide × 14″ deep × 16″ tall, **$135.**

Child's open-weave wicker rocker, flat arms, upholstered seat, 19″ wide × 23″ tall, **$135.**

Brimfield, Massachusetts (each May, July and September), and Renninger's Extravaganza in Kutztown, Pennsylvania (held each April, June and September), draw thousands of dealers and have become world renowned, with both drawing collectors from Europe and Canada.

Monthly flea markets such as the Ann Arbor, Michigan, Antiques Market; Don Scott Antique Market in Columbus, Ohio; and the Kane County Antique Flea Markets at the Kane County Fairgrounds in St. Charles, Illinois, are just a few examples of the popular markets that have become well known and respected and draw record crowds. There are also weekly flea markets held all across the country.

Annual and semiannual antiques shows are another avenue to explore for country furniture, and many dealers will save a special piece specifically for this antiques show. One popular annual event is the Madison-Bouckville Antique Show, held one August weekend each year in the Madison-Bouckville, New York, region. This event features 1000 antiques dealers and is always well attended.

When visiting these outdoor shows, comfortable walking shoes are a must, as well as sunscreen, a hat, and an umbrella or rain poncho just in case. It's a good idea to carry a small measuring tape, pocket flashlight, and cash or personal checks since many dealers do not accept credit cards.

SECTION III
Country Furniture Close Up

In the beginning, the small, single-room dwellings the settlers built in the Northeast, the adobe homes the Spaniards built in the Southwest, and the early log cabins that dotted the interior of the country were furnished with just a few simple pieces of furniture. Many of the colonists, and later the settlers that crossed the country, were only able to carry with them a trunk or blanket chest containing their few worldly possessions. As a result, their early homes were sparsely furnished with a blanket chest and the necessary handmade pieces that could serve dual purposes, such as a settle that could also be used as a bed.

The eighteenth century saw the dawn of ethnic diversity in American country furniture. Populated centers along the Eastern Seaboard still looked to England and Europe for their sense of style, and had skilled craftsmen create their furnishings accordingly (or had their furniture brought over from England). The rest of the new land witnessed the birth of a culturally rich American furniture style that accompanied the various groups of immigrants—Swedes, Pennsylvania Dutch and Shakers—as they settled in the more remote areas.

A home in a well-populated area stood in sharp contrast to the home of the wilderness settler. In towns and growing cities or seaports, the eighteenth-century home was light and colorful. Walls were often decorated with expensive French wallpaper and rooms were carefully furnished with pieces based on English styles. During this period, the corner cupboard became popular for displaying fine pieces of china, highboys stored the family linens, and Windsors and slat-backs provided the seating. Large hutches were used in the kitchens for storage, dishes, and other necessities.

In rural areas the settlers often decorated their walls, too, sometimes using paint and a sponge to achieve a patterned look. Folk artists traveled from town to town, painting scenes on the interior walls of homes in exchange for a meal and a place to sleep. Some of them used stencils, while others painted freehand. The furniture in these early homes combined necessity and ingenuity. It usually was built by the farmer to serve a definite purpose (or two) and sometimes was crafted and/or decorated to fit a specific spot in the house.

Although numerous country pieces were constructed throughout the eighteenth century, it is the early nineteenth century which is considered to be the high point for American country furniture. Following the dictates of city style and fashion, many country pieces were painted or grained to imitate the then-popular furniture of urban centers. Country craftsmen often poured heart and soul into their work, turning out spectacular one-of-a-kind furniture pieces.

During the 1700s settlers also painted the utilitarian pine pieces they crafted. This was the most available means of adding a dash of color to a plain and simple room, and at the same time it served to protect the wood.

Painted Furniture

During the early seventeenth century, handcrafted country furniture pieces were usually painted a red-brown, brown or black, and later blue, green, gray or ochre became common. Along with protecting the wood, paint would give the piece a uniform appearance. Color was extracted from berries, vegetable matter, or clays and mixed with water, skim milk, or linseed oil. For example, black was achieved from mixing the soot in the chimney (once washed and ground) with linseed oil; reds were created not just from berries but also from a powder made of iron oxide which could produce red-brown, light red, and even a shade of maroon. An early blue was created by heating a combination of iron, iron oxide, potash, organic materials, and sand. This "Prussian blue" is considered to be the very first artificial color pigment. Shades of green, including a dark green (terre verte) and a light green (verdegris), could be made from the patina which forms on both brass and copper.

While many of these early pieces were simply painted, others were given elaborate folk-art decorations of multicolored hearts, stars, and other patterns.

During the eighteenth century country craftsmen were using feathers, combs, sponges and crinkled paper to add an ornamental graining or swirl design to a painted country piece. This was more often than not an artistic measure or decorative touch, and not an imitation of formal furniture (as it was later on), for houses too incorporated more and more color in both walls and flooring. As settlers and immigrants continued to spread across the land and communities began to take root, prosper and grow, a blossoming interest in adding color and decorative touches to homes developed.

The early 1800s was a time of great expansion in America. Immigrants continued to pour into the country and settlers pushed further west. As they set-

Primitive pine doughbox with old red paint, 38" wide × 18" deep × 34" tall, **$350.**

Child's chair with original blue paint, 15" wide × 14" deep × 24" tall, **$125.**

Step-back cupboard, red painted finish, two small drawers, **$2000–$2500.** Photo courtesy of *AntiqueWeek*.

properly conducted and varnished, has a most beautiful appearance, and is less likely to meet with injury than japanning."

Moore's publication included the following recipes:

> *To make a black stain: Take one pound of logwood, boil it in four quarts of water, add a double handful of walnut peeling, boil it up again, take out the chips, add a pint of the best vinegar, and it will be fit for use; apply it boiling hot.*
>
> *To stain beechwood a mahogany color: Take two ounces of dragon's blood, break it in pieces and put it into a quart of rectified spirits of wine; let the bottle stand in*

tled, they of course built, or had built, those furniture pieces needed for their frontier homes. Cabinetmakers that traveled to the rural areas had to make their own paints and stains, and while recipes for paint were easy to come by (most households had a recipe or two and domestic life publications or farm journals often included directions on making paints), mixing stains or making varnish was another story. As a result, numerous small publications sprang into existence to offer advice on furniture finishing to the country craftsman.

The Cabinet-Makers' Guide, written by Jacob B. Moore of Concord, New Hampshire, in 1827, instructed readers as follows, "staining differs from the process of dy[e]ing in as much as it penetrates just below the surface of the wood, instead of colouring its substance throughout. . . . staining is chiefly in use among chairmakers, and when

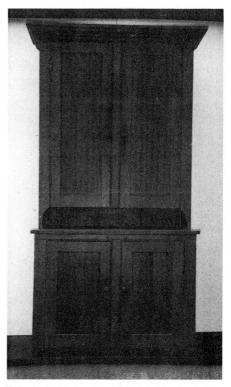

Tall pine step-back cupboard with decorative green paint in door panels, **$2000–$2500.** Photo courtesy of *AntiqueWeek*.

a warm place, shake it frequently, and when dissolved it is fit for use.

To imitate rosewood: Take half a pound of logwood, boil it with three pints of water till it is of a very dark red, to which add about half an ounce of salt of tartar, and when boiling hot stain your wood with two or three coats, taking care that it is nearly dry between each; then with a stiff flat brush, such as is used by the painters for graining, form streaks with black stain, which if carefully executed, will be very near the appearance of dark rose-wood.

Staining and graining furniture to achieve the look of more costly woods was very popular through the early nineteenth century both as decoration and as an attempt to create "finery" such as those in stylish urban centers enjoyed.

Country craftsmen, folk artists and skilled cabinetmakers all practiced furniture painting and graining, and today some collectors categorize painted furniture as plain, imaginative and imitative. "Plain" refers to a piece painted in just one color, with no decorations in a contrasting color or graining, sponging, combing, or other ornamentation. Plainly painted furniture pieces were usually made by rural craftsmen and farmers.

Imaginative painting—cultural motifs, lifelike scenes, or appealing de-

Small tool chest with original green paint, lid has initials L.F.F. in red, 30½″ wide × 14″ deep × 13″ tall, **$110.**

Pine blanket box with original green paint, rope handles, 34″ wide × 16″ deep × 15″ tall, **$235.**

Hints on Painted Furniture

Old paint has a patina that is the result of years of exposure to air, dirt, and wear and will have a faded look, possibly with spots where the paint has been worn off entirely or has chipped or crazed. Make sure, however, that worn areas and wear marks make sense because steel wool can easily create the same effect.

Try to examine a painted piece either outdoors where sunlight will betray new paint and touched-up areas, or under strong light indoors. A flashlight is handy for checking those areas that would not originally have been painted, such as drawer bottoms and sides, underneath the skirt, or on the backing. Remember that farmers and country craftsmen did not have time to paint those areas not readily visible.

Reproduction painted pieces and fake finishes on authentic pieces exist. An original finish or very old paint hardens with time and becomes brittle. If scraped, it will fall like a powder. New/fake paint will come off in curly ribbons or pieces.

Mid–nineteenth century washstand, painted mustard yellow with brown trim, 17″ wide × 14″ deep × 34″ tall, **$295.**

Pennsylvania dry sink/cupboard, circa 1830–1850, original mustard paint, 42″ wide × 77″ tall, **price not available.**

Early pine cupboard with old mustard paint, door hinges have been replaced over the years, 38" wide × 14½" deep × 60" tall, **$275.**

Pine cupboard, old blue-gray paint, five shelves inside, 48" wide × 17½" deep × 76" tall, **$350.**

Grain-painted cupboard from Massachusetts, 44" wide × 17" deep × 54" tall, **$850.**

Pine two-door cupboard, circa 1830, old green paint with blue on each door panel, 45" wide × 14" deep × 62" tall, **$1575.**

signs—often was done by the rural craftsman or folk artist over the paint.

Imitative painted furniture combined colors and employed the use of combs, sponges, and other effects to achieve the look of a more costly wood grain. Imitative pieces were created by rural craftsmen with varying degrees of skill.

Today's collector will find that authentic painted furniture pieces are becoming harder to find and are costly, with large cupboards being the most expensive. Along with supply and demand factors, keep in mind that age and quality (of both construction and finish) will affect pricing.

Beds, Bedroom Furniture and Cradles

Long before the country home had a separate bedroom, the bed was a necessary piece of furniture and an integral part of the multipurpose one-room structure. Some early homes included a loft for sleeping, but the majority delegated a corner of the room to the family bed or beds.

During the 1600s settlers made use of simple wooden frames for their beds.

During the 1700s, as homes began to have rooms specifically for sleeping, beds of mortise and tenon construction became larger and often had canopies and curtains to protect the occupants from the cold night air. Rope was used to support the mattress in place.

Today's country furniture collector looks to the nineteenth and early twentieth centuries, which ushered in a vari-

Spool crib, 47″ long × 27″ wide × 23″ tall, **$295.**

Pine crib, 37″ long × 21″ wide × 30″ tall, **$495.**

Jenny Lind spool bed, headboard and footboard, double bed size, 54″ wide × 40″ tall, **$149.**

ety of styles and designs in beds along with changes in construction methods. Several different types of low-post beds were popular during the 1800s, including the cannonball bed, Shaker low-post bed, sleigh bed (so called because its lines resembled a horse-drawn sleigh), and the Jenny Lind spool bed

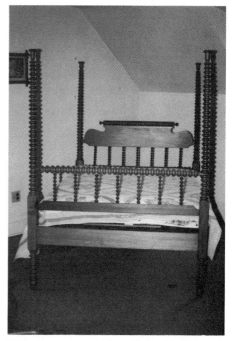

High poster spool bed, early to mid-nineteenth century, **$1500–$2000. Photo courtesy of** An-tiqueWeek.

Washstand with spool turnings on legs and towel bars, scalloped bottom shelf, **$300–$500.** Photo courtesy of *AntiqueWeek*.

Birch wardrobe with glass insert in center door, knocks down for easy moving, 56″ wide × 23″ deep × 78″ tall, **price not available.**

(named after famous nineteenth-century actress Jenny Lind, who reportedly slept in a spool bed).

Many of these beds were constructed with mortise and tenon joints and ropes to hold the mattress, but others, especially the spool bed, were made with screws and wooden slats.

Early spool beds (1830–1850) were made with straight lines, while those produced after 1850 had headboards and footboards with curved corners. The Jenny Lind spool bed was one of the first country furniture products of the Industrial Revolution and was in fact produced at many different factories because of the development of a new lathe. This tool could make fancy turnings that were cut and used to spool sewing thread. Initially, the extra spiral-

Pine wardrobe with bun feet, 44″ wide × 18″ deep × 75″ tall, **$595.**

Quartered Oak Veneer—Serpentine Front

$26⁸⁵
Quartered
Oak
Top and
Front

$26⁹⁵
Dresser

$26⁶⁵
Quartered
Oak
Veneer

Rich Golden Finish

Serpentine Front

Shaped Mirror

Princess Dresser, beautifully veneered with Quartered Oak on top, front and sides, with an attractive serpentine front. Finished a rich Golden. Top, 19 by 36 inches; adjustable plate mirror, 16 by 30 inches. Height, 70 inches. Easy rolling casters. Shipping weight, about 150 pounds.
166 F 4742.................$26.85

Beautiful Dresser of seasoned hardwood with Quartered Oak veneer on top, front and sides. It is finished a rich Golden. The sturdy frame is rigidly blocked and reinforced at all the joints. Serpentine front. Top, 19 by 40 inches, adjustable plate mirror, 18 by 22 inches. Easy rolling casters. Shipping weight, about 125 pounds.
166 F 4740.................$26.95

This beautiful Chiffonier of select hardwood, veneered with genuine Quartered Oak, will look well in most any bedroom. Golden finish. Has five extra large drawers, round wood pulls. Top, 19 by 32 inches; fitted with adjustable plate mirror, 16 by 20 inches. Easy rolling casters. Shipping weight, about 135 pounds.
166 F 4741.................$26.65

Ad from a 1924 Montgomery Ward catalog.

One-drawer pine washstand, unusual design with cross piece on bottom to support a water pitcher, circa 1880, 30″ wide, 16″ deep × 32″ tall, **$225.**

Makes a Dainty Bedroom at Low Cost

A 1918 Montgomery Ward catalog ad.

shaped pieces of wood were used for furniture making, but before long the new shape was being produced specifically for the beds, tables, chairs, washstands, and other furnishings that had become so popular with the middle class.

Spool furniture was featured in an 1849 issue of the magazine *Godey's Lady's Book,* when Lydia Maria Hale, author of a column called the "Cottage Furniture Department," included line drawings of spool furnishings and noted ideas on their use in the home. This

43

Full-size brass bed, sold at auction for **$300**; and walnut two-piece step-back cupboard with 6-pane (3 × 3) upper doors and old blue paint inside, sold at auction for **$850**. Photo courtesy of *AntiqueWeek*.

particular style of mass-produced furnishings remained popular until the late 1800s.

Another common factory-made bedroom furniture produced during the nineteenth century was known as cottage furniture, and while spool furniture is often included in this category, the two are being described individually for the purposes of this book.

In 1850, noted designer and landscape architect Andrew Jackson Downing wrote *The Architecture of Country Houses,* in which he recommended "chaste, simple and expressive" furniture. His book included designs for cozy country cottages, and he advised furnishing them with attractive painted pieces.

Most cottage furniture was made for the bedroom. Pine, poplar and/or birchwood pieces were constructed with early machine-made dovetail joints or nails and glue. They were then painted in pastel shades of blue, pink, green, purple, gray or white. Women and children were employed to hand-paint imitative graining, floral decora-

tions, and landscape scenes or stencil stripes, scrolls, vines, and other designs.

Cottage furniture became popular not just in the summer homes of the wealthy, but also in furnishing the homes of the growing middle class. It was affordable (a top-of-the-line eight piece bedroom outfit cost $100 in 1850), attractive, stylish and readily available. Cottage furniture continued to be made until the early 1900s, at which time factory-made oak furnishings became more popular.

Brass beds and iron beds were introduced in the late nineteenth century, and conveniently could be bought through mail-order catalogs from the 1890s until the early 1900s. While some examples were highly decorated, others were made with simple straight lines or modest ornamentation. For example, the 1895 Montgomery Ward and Company's Catalog No. 57 offered their least expensive iron bed for $4.80 and advertised it as "iron bed, extra good value and a bargain. This bed is made of all iron with brass knobs, size of posts 1 inch. Finished in white enamel, well made and cheap, will guar-

Cherry spool washstand, 24″ wide × 30″ tall, **$285**.

One-drawer pine washstand with towel bars, old brown paint, 40″ wide × 16″ deep × 36″ tall, **$495.**

antee satisfaction. Size 4′6″ wide by 6′6″ long and weight 100 pounds." Slats had to be ordered separately and cost an additional 35 cents.

By 1897 brass beds also were included in Montgomery Ward's catalogs and were much more expensive than the iron beds. A simple design of the same size as the iron bed described previously was $23.50.

Other necessary nineteenth-century bedroom furnishings included the wardrobe, commode and washstand.

Since most homes built during the 1800s lacked closets, the wardrobe, a descendant of the eighteenth-century linen press, was an important piece of furniture used to store clothing and linens. Most were constructed of pine, poplar, walnut or cherry and they often were painted. Many wardrobes were constructed in sections so they could be taken apart and moved. Inside are

Tiger maple washstand with backsplash, sold at auction for **$800.** Photo courtesy of *AntiqueWeek.*

Hints on Beds, Bedroom Furniture and Cradles

Remember that early nineteenth century beds used rope to hold the mattress in place, and that slats were introduced during the second half of the century.

Carefully examine the finish on cottage furniture to determine whether it is authentic or a reproduction.

Straight lines on a spool bed indicate that it was made prior to 1850, while curves and angles note later manufacture.

Washstands are not hard to come by, however, corner washstands are scarce. Look them over carefully to determine sound construction, and if painted, an original finish.

The original paint on iron beds is usually in poor condition. Repainting will not harm the value of this piece *unless* it is poorly done.

Pine commode, 30" wide × 15½" deep × 29" tall, **$165.**

Lift-top commode with grain and sponge painting, 28" wide × 17" deep × 30" tall, **$365.**

shelves for storage, pegs for hanging clothes, and sometimes a storage drawer at the bottom.

Until plumbing was brought indoors during the late 1800s, the washstand and commode were needed for daily washing and storing the chamber pot. Washstands were made in different shapes and sizes from the 1840s through the 1890s. Both rectangular and corner washstands were made with a hole cut in the top to accommodate a wash basin and a shelf underneath for toiletries. Other washstands were made more like a table; the basin and water pitcher sat on top. These washstands often had towel bars on either side. Many were made of pine and often were painted.

Lift-top commodes were also used

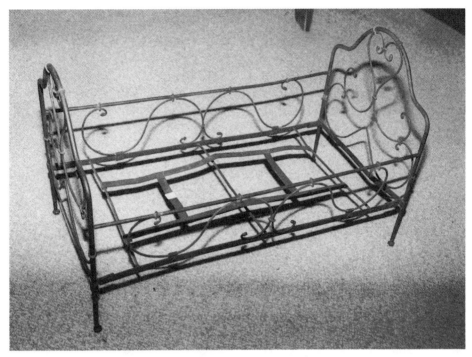

Doll's iron bed, painted green, 25″ long × 13″ wide × 16″ tall, **$175.**

Primitive pine cradle, 35″ long × 14″ wide × 15½″ tall, **$167.**

Baby cradle, painted white with high hooded back, 38″ long × 14″ wide × 28″ tall, **$265.**

for the washbowl and pitcher (which were stored in a compartment with a lift-top lid), and the chamber pot was tucked away behind a small cupboard door. These, too, were often made of pine or other soft woods and were frequently painted.

Baby cradles were among the earliest country pieces made and very early examples were plain and boxlike. These cradles were constructed of boards on small rockers, and a hood was often added later on. Other cradles were made with a tall headboard and footboard, and this particular style remained popular through the nineteenth century. More decorative examples made during the 1800s had scallop designs, were painted, or had small openings cut out on either side to allow the cradle to be carried.

Cupboards and Factory-Made Cabinets

During the seventeenth century open shelves were used for storing dishes, cups and plates. As time passed shelves were encased and the "cup board," as the open shelves were called, became a "cupboard." A common cupboard form during both the 1700s and 1800s was the piece constructed with two sections. A top piece with open or enclosed shelves (blind-front doors were used until glass panes were introduced around 1850), sat on a bottom section that might have drawers for additional storage or another shelf or two behind wooden cupboard doors. Cupboards were constructed freestanding or built-in, paneled and dovetailed or nailed, with a plain or decorative cornice. While some cupboards were made of hardwoods, most were made of pine and therefore painted blue, red, green, brown or gray.

A cupboard built with open shelving on top is often referred to as a pewter cupboard, but in one variation of the typical cupboard form, European influence inspired the hutch or Welsh dresser (an older, larger version with recessed open shelves on top). This influence gives the upper shelves a step-back appearance and allows for much-needed counter space. Rather than a storage area underneath, the early hutch had high legs and two or three drawers. Later examples of the step-back included more drawers and/or a cupboard door on the bottom.

Pine pewter cupboard, 54″ wide × 18″ deep × 76″ tall, **$1400.**

Blind-front cupboard with old blue paint over red, 38″ wide × 15″ deep × 70″ tall, **$475.**

Step-back painted cupboard, tan with green interior, 46″ wide × 82″ tall, **$850.**

Another popular cupboard was the corner cupboard. These were first constructed during the late 1600s and were very often found in the eighteenth-century parlor to display whatever pieces of china or pewter the family might have. Since they were often built-in, corner cupboards featured one-piece construction, were built right on the floor (hence, there are no feet on these cupboards) and usually had fancy moldings. In early cupboards the enclosed space on the bottom frequently had decorative door panels, but these disappeared by the nineteenth century as corner cupboard design became plain and simple. They were constructed of whatever wood was readily available, including pine, poplar, cherry, apple, maple, walnut, butternut, or a combination of a hardwood with a secondary wood (typically pine or poplar). During the late 1700s and early 1800s, it was common practice to paint corner cupboards so that they matched the color of the walls in the parlor or dining room in which they were built in.

Corner cupboards built during the second half of the nineteenth century often had glass-paneled doors and were used primarily in the kitchen. They were very basic in design and frequently were left with a natural wood finish. Blind-front or solid wood cupboard doors were also used on some corner versions built specifically for storage and not for display, as were many eighteenth-century cupboards.

Another early cupboard of built-in construction is the chimney cupboard. This cupboard is so-called because it most often was built into the wall next to the kitchen or keeping room fireplace during the eighteenth and early nine-

49

teenth centuries. It was used to store cooking pots and other kitchen necessities.

Chimney cupboards are quite tall and narrow, and most examples have both a top and bottom cupboard door (although the earliest examples were crafted with just one long door). Most chimney cupboards are plain, but some were given decorative moldings and panels on the cupboard doors and painted to blend in with the rest of the wall around the fireplace.

The nineteenth-century household required several different types of cupboards to serve many purposes, and later in the century, factory-made cupboards continued to serve as food storage, preparation and preservation centers.

One such cupboard, the pie safe, was made after the 1830s to store per-ishables such as meat, milk, cheese and butter, along with the home-baked pies and breads. Built on tall legs, pie safes protected the food from insects and rodents, while at the same time allowing air to circulate by way of the fabric, screen or pierced-tin panels in the door or doors and sometimes the sides of the cupboard. Pie safes were made in a variety of sizes, no doubt determined by the size of the kitchens they were intended for, and both one- and two-door examples can be found. The pie safe was a "working piece," and therefore crafted of whatever wood or woods were readily available. The majority of them were then painted. Those with original punched tin inserts (in good condition, with very decorative panels adding a great deal more to the value of the cupboard) are the most sought-after examples today.

Open cupboard with old blue-green paint, 36″ wide × 13″ deep × 70″ tall, **$785.**

Open cupboard with four shelves, painted green, 35½″ wide × 14″ deep × 60″ tall, **$550.**

White Enameled Chair $2.98

White enameled Chair for kitchen or breakfast room. Made of Hardwood and finished attractively in enamel. Low, comfortable back. Seat, 15½ by 15½ inches. Shipping weight, about 12 pounds.
166 F 3008 .... $2.98

$16.95

taken apart to save you freight. Shipping weight, about 100 pounds.
166 F 4025 .... $16.95

Kitchen Cupboard Art Glass Doors

There is no reason why you should not have good-looking furniture in your kitchen, for it is there you spend about ¼ of your time. This Cabinet is very handsome with its art glass doors and careful finish. Ample space is provided for those articles in every day use which means a saving of many steps and considerable time. Open doors show arrangement of shelves in upper compartment. Very handy for use of the many odd utensils often in use way in other places. Built of Hardwood, with solid Oak front. Finished Golden. Two shelves, two drawers, cupboard. Entire height, 74 inches. Width, 38 inches. Shipped taken apart. Shipping weight, about 100 pounds.

$9.95

Kitchen Cupboard

Made of seasoned Hardwood, finished Golden. Has one large drawer at the top. Compartment contain two adjustable shelves. Height, 60 inches; width, 34 inches. Shipped taken apart. Shipping weight, about 70 pounds.
166 F 4028 .... $9.95

Kitchen Cupboard Glass Doors

How much more pleasant is your kitchen work when you have such a convenient Cupboard with a place provided for utensils in every day use. Built of hardwood with Oak front, finished Golden. Two shelves, two drawers and cupboard provide ample space for your kitchen utensils, chinaware, cutlery, groceries and in fact, everything you need in preparing a meal. Shelf in lower space increases storage space 50 per cent and makes a convenient place for many bulky articles. Clear glass doors keeps your groceries and utensils safe from dust, yet enables you to see at a glance, just what supplies you have on hand. Entire height, 78 inches; width, 38 inches. Shipped taken apart to save you freight, about 100 pounds.
166 F 4022 .... $14.95

$14.95

Ad from a 1924 Montgomery Ward catalog.

Another cupboard no nineteenth-century country kitchen could do without was the jelly or jam cupboard. This piece was used to store the homemade preserves and keep precious spices, tea and sugar. Jelly cupboards were often considered more than just working pieces or storage cupboards, since they housed valuable spices and could be found in the dining room as well as the kitchen. Simple examples were made from pine or poplar and were painted in the popular red, gray, blue or green. Jelly cupboards crafted for the dining room were often made from walnut or cherry and have moldings, attractive paneled doors, and brass or iron latches on the cupboard door. Those examples with one or two drawers on top have wooden, brass or porcelain knobs.

The growing Industrial Revolution of the nineteenth century impacted upon the kitchen of the late 1800s in several ways. Along with the flood of patented gadgets to make food preparation easier, a free-standing storage/ work area was designed. The factory-made baker's cupboard of the 1890s grew from the simple baker's table (a worktable with two drawers and one or two possum-belly bin drawers for flour or corn meal underneath). A top section

Factory-made oak two-piece step-back cupboard with pie shelf, glass cupboard doors, sold at auction for **$750**. Photo courtesy of *AntiqueWeek*.

Corner cupboard, 16-pane (8 × 8) glass doors, **$2500–$3000**. Photo courtesy of *AntiqueWeek*.

Baker's cupboard, refinished with mustard color milk paint, 46″ wide × 26″ deep × 63″ tall, **$775**.

Poplar two-drawer jelly cupboard, 45″ wide × 16″ deep × 50″ tall, **$495**.

Primitive jelly cupboard, pine with white and green over old red paint, 37½″ wide × 13½″ deep × 60″ tall, **$235**.

Pine jelly cupboard with ornate brass latch, 44" wide × 17" deep × 59" tall, **$695.**

Cherry corner cupboard, 12-pane (6 × 6) glass doors, scalloped skirt, **$2600–$3200.** Photo courtesy of *AntiqueWeek*.

Canadian-made baker's cupboard, pine with old red over green paint, glass inserts in top cupboard doors, 46" wide × 28" deep × 70" tall, **$1950.**

Corner cupboard with blind-front paneled doors, **$1400–$1800.** Photo courtesy of *AntiqueWeek*.

Cherry corner cabinet with 12-pane (6 × 6) glass doors, small center drawer, 82″ tall, sold at auction for **$2900**. Photo courtesy of *AntiqueWeek*.

Corner cupboard with four blind-front paneled doors, mid–nineteenth century, **$2200–$2600**. Photo courtesy of *AntiqueWeeks*.

Early walnut corner cupboard, 16-pane (8 × 8) glass doors, detailed moldings and scalloped shelves, sold at auction for **$1950**. Photo courtesy of *AntiqueWeek*.

was eventually added, made up of multiple small spice drawers and perhaps a small cupboard or two. Baker's cupboards were constructed of maple, pine, oak or elm in a variety of sizes and styles. Top-of-the-line models often had etched glass inserts in top cupboard doors, and most models were made with a wooden work surface. Their popularity sprang from their convenience and ability to save the housewife numerous steps back and forth across the kitchen (they served as a pantry of sorts). This lead to continued design development, and resulted in the hoosier kitchen cabinet.

The hoosier cabinet was factory made from the late 1890s through the 1930s. Hoosiers (regardless of manufacturer, all such cabinets are generically referred to by that name) were pro-

Hoosier Mfg. oak cabinet complete with flour and sugar bins, carousel spice rack, glass canisters, grocery and meal planning lists, 41″ wide × 69″ tall, **$1200.**

Cherry boot-jack blanket box, circa 1830, 39″ wide × 18″ deep × 22″ tall, **$595.**

Pine blanket box with original green paint, 34″ long × 16″ deep × 15″ tall, **$235.**

Plank-seat rocker, traces of old red paint, 15″ wide × 15″ deep × 32″ tall, **$165.**

Youth chair, pine with old brown paint, 11″ wide × 12″ deep × 32″ tall, **$58.**

Golden oak school desk with attached seat (seat has drawer), 21″ wide × 14″ deep × 31″ tall, **$190.**

Shaker rocker from Mount Lebanon, tape seat, 21″ wide × 18″ deep × 42″ tall, **$1275.**

Cherry one-drawer stand with tapered legs, 22″ wide × 18″ deep × 28″ tall, **$295.**

Oak ball and stick parlor table, 30″ wide × 24″ deep x 27″ tall, **$185.**

Maple rocker, seat replaced in 1960s, 16″ wide × 36″ tall, **$90.**

White wicker chair with magazine holder on arm, 33″ wide × 24″ deep × 40″ tall, **$195.**

Metal porch chair, circa 1930s, 19″ wide × 20″ deep × 35″ tall, **$40.**

Primitive rope day bed, 74″ long × 24″ wide × 10″ tall, **$425.**

Oak Hoosier Manufacturing Company cabinet with flour bin, carousel spice rack, tambour doors, 40½″ wide × 70″ tall, **$895.**

This full-page color ad from an early 1920s magazine boasted about the many benefits of owning a hoosier. A prolific advertising campaign made the 1920s the peak years of production and sales.

Oak hoosier cabinet, 40″ wide × 70″ tall, **$700.**

duced by several different companies, including the Hoosier Manufacturing Company of New Castle, Indiana; Mutschler Brothers Company of Nappanee, Indiana; Showers Brothers Company of Bloomington, Indiana; McDougall Company of Frankfort, Indiana; G.I. Sellers and Sons of Elwood, Indiana; and the Campbell-Smith-Ritchie Company of Lebanon, Indiana (maker of Boone cabinets).

The Hoosier Manufacturing Company was by far the leader in production of these all-purpose "helpmates," followed closely by G. I. Sellers and Sons. While they both turned out cabinets in various styles and sizes, all cabinets were basically the same—a two-piece unit with a wooden, zinc or modern porce-

Pie safe, 16 tins with star design, single drawer below, 78″ tall, **$1400–$1600.** Photo courtesy of *AntiqueWeek.*

Punched-tin pie safe with two drawers, cherry front and top, 41″ wide × 14″ deep × 54″ tall, **$550.**

Punched-tin pie safe with old blue paint, 41″ wide × 16″ deep × 53″ tall, **$350.**

Punched-tin pie safe, **$600–$800.** Photo courtesy of *AntiqueWeek.*

Punched-tin pine pie safe, two top drawers, **$800–$1000.** Photo courtesy of *AntiqueWeek.*

Small pie safe with screen, old mustard over red paint, 30½" wide × 16" deep × 34" tall, **$275.**

Early six-tin pie cupboard in original finish, one drawer and two closed cupboard doors underneath, sold at auction for **$350.** Photo courtesy of *AntiqueWeek.*

A Sellers and Sons oak hoosier with slag glass inserts in top cupboard doors, porcelain-enamel work top, drawers have glass knobs, 42" wide × 70" tall, **$650.**

A child's oak kitchen cupboard in original condition, 25″ wide × 14″ deep × 50″ tall, **$625.**

Primitive cupboard, white with a halfmoon painted on the door, four shelves inside, 37″ wide × 14″ deep × 72″ tall, **$175.**

lain-enamel work surface; and a bottom section with silverware drawer(s), storage area behind a bottom cupboard door, and three or four drawers (one of which was usually tin-lined for bread). Hoosier cabinet top sections include a storage cupboard for dishware, a tin flour bin with sifter that was always located on the left, a spice shelf or revolving spice carousel (on Hoosier Manufacturing Company models), and a sugar jar and canisters that were often concealed behind a roll-top door.

Nationally advertised as a concentrated work center that would bring modernization to the kitchen, all hoosier cabinets were designed to provide for a woman's every need when baking or preparing meals. Standard features

Cherry two-drawer cupboard, nailed construction, 32″ wide × 18″ deep × 38″ tall, **$1150.**

Small pine cupboard, painted black, one drawer and door with porcelain knob, 30″ wide × 16″ deep × 28″ tall, **$180.**

Child's homemade cupboard, back inscribed "W. Synder, Pittston," painted red, 31″ wide × 15″ deep × 48″ tall, **$275.**

included plenty of storage space, a flour bin/sifter, pull-out bread boards, recipe box, reminder lists, canister sets, and much-needed work room provided by a pull-out extension top.

Early cabinets were available in an oak finish or painted white enamel, such as the "Good Fairy" model available through the 1924 Montgomery Ward catalog. For $43.95 (in golden oak finish), a housewife could have the "Good Fairy," which Montgomery Ward claimed would "save thousands of steps in dozens of convenient ways." The catalog went on to ask,

> *Did you ever stop to figure how many steps a woman takes each day? And that thousands of these steps could be saved with the proper kitchen equipment? If you are still keeping the house the old, round-about, pantry-to-table-to-cupboard way, we want you to consider seriously what this Good Fairy will do for you. It will cut you steps in half! This Good Fairy Master-Made Kitchen Cabinet is meant for women who demand the best . . . .*

Pine cupboard, wainscotted, two glass doors, 42″ wide × 11½″ deep × 51″ tall, **$395.**

Advertisement from the 1918 Montgomery Ward catalog.

A Cabinet Makes Your Day's Work Lighter and Shorter $26⁸⁵ Metal Top

No longer need the cost of a Kitchen Cabinet prevent you from enjoying its many conveniences—get one of these latest models at this remarkably low price. It is a practical convenience which should be in your kitchen because it will save you so much time and so many steps. It is arranged to bring almost everything you need within a space smaller than your kitchen table. You can prepare your meals with a great deal less work and in much less time. After you have had it a short time you will never want to be without it. Besides, it will give you more time to do other things.

Sturdily built of well seasoned oak; sliding top of white porcelain or nickeled metal. You will have plenty of room for dishes, bowls and jars in the china closet. Rolling curtain front is sanitary and perfectly dustproof. Tilting glass sugar jar and scoop and five spice jars on rack. Large size tilting flour bin on left side has metal sifter. Jars for tea and coffee on rack of flour bin door. Sliding top can be pulled out—gives you a space 40 inches long and 36 inches wide to do your work on. Under the sliding top is cutting board which pulls out with top. Block for attaching meat chopper on right side of sliding top. In the bottom are two drawers where you can keep cutlery and the many other small things you need in your work in the kitchen. The large drawer at bottom has metal bread and cake box with sliding metal lid. Base cupboard has sliding metal shelf and pan rack. Three-ply bottom base with substantially built frame work. Groceries and dishes in cupboard and utensils in lower section are not included in our low price. They are illustrated only to show how convenient it will be for you to use this cabinet. Height, 68 inches. Width, 40 inches. Depth, 25 inches. Shipping weight, 220 pounds.

166 F 4129—With Metal top.................$26.85
166 F 4130—With Porcelain top.............. 30.85

Approximate Freight Charges on Kitchen Cabinets

Weight	150 Miles	300 Miles	500 Miles
200 pounds	$1.60	$2.70	$3.50
225 pounds	1.80	3.05	3.95
240 pounds	1.95	3.25	4.25
300 pounds	2.40	4.05	5.25

For exact shipping charges to your station, turn to Page 315

A 1924 Montgomery Ward catalog page.

Unusual pine cupboard found in a law office, 38″ wide × 18″ deep × 73″ tall, **price unavailable.**

Interior of previously shown pine cupboard, showing shelves and cubbyholes that no doubt stored files and supplies.

Extremely tall corner cupboard, pine, four blind-front paneled cupboard doors, **$2000–$2500**. Photo courtesy of *AntiqueWeek*.

Pine kitchen cupboard, originally a built-in, glass doors and brass pulls, 48″ wide × 79″ tall, **$300**.

Hoosier cabinets were sold at furniture stores and through mail-order catalogs. From 1900 through 1920 deluxe models were available with frosted glass or slag glass inserts in cupboard doors. The Art Deco hoosier of the late 1920s and the 1930s often had geometric stenciled designs on cupboard doors and was available in a wide array of enamel finishes such as gold, ivory, green and gray.

Because a hoosier cabinet was actually a piece of kitchen furniture, many companies offered their customers membership in a "club" through their local furniture store where they could put $1.00 down, take a hoosier home, and just pay $1.00 a week until the balance was paid. A 1925 magazine ad for the Hoosier Manufacturing Company's Hoosier Highboy model told readers,

Time was, when the kitchen was the "ugly duckling" of the house. That was before women realized how vastly much difference our surroundings make in the way we do our work . . . the kitchen should be as cheerful and charming as your living room; completely, efficiently furnished. . . . Your kitchen may be old but it does not need to be old fashioned . . . . The Hoosier Company has an Easy Payment Plan whereby you select the unit you need

Hints on Country Cupboards and Factory-Made Cabinets

Perhaps no other piece of country furniture exhibits so much American craftsmanship as the cupboard. There are so many variations in style, decorative touches and finishes. Generally, keep in mind that wide-board construction was used early on and it wasn't until later in the nineteenth century that cupboard backs were made of smaller, equally sized boards. An early nineteenth century cupboard should have a backing of random-width wide boards.

Closely examine the patina of an old cupboard. Wood exposed to air, light, dirt and dust will discolor over time and become a mellow shade of brown. Be suspicious of a piece exhibiting wide variations in its coloring, as this could indicate replacement parts or a piece made up of assorted old woods.

Examine the construction of the cupboard, and be sure to inspect the hardware/nails for telltale signs of age.

Those cupboards with old glass-paned doors are today fetching higher prices than a blind-front cupboard. Check glass inserts carefully for evidence of new wood around the panes, alterations, and other repairs or replacements. Remember that the old glass used in cupboard doors has a wavy appearance, but some cupboards are bound to have a replacement pane or two as odds are some glass will have broken over the years. (Note that reproductions are currently being made with wavy glass.)

Regarding old pie safes, these working pieces often took a beating and the original screening or punched tin literally may have been destroyed. Carefully consider the size and style (any unusual features?) and examine the finish as original paint in good condition is most desirable. A pie safe with replacement punched tin is not worth as much as an example with the original tin in good condition. Keep in mind that old tin dulls with time and does not have a shiny appearance.

When looking at hoosier cabinets, an example with the flour bin/sifter is worth $100 more than a cabinet without one. Etched glass or slag glass inserts increase the value of a hoosier, as does an original wood finish. While the enamel-painted hoosier originally cost more brand new than those with a plain wood finish, today we find demand has created the opposite effect, resulting in higher prices for those with a wood (especially oak) finish. Remember that those cabinets originally painted at the factory were usually made from a combination of woods (since they were going to be painted), and are not necessarily attractive if stripped of their painted finish.

and enjoy it in your kitchen at once. Just a small downpayment brings them; take your time about paying the balance.

The free-standing hoosier kitchen cabinet had its heyday during the 1920s, peak years of production for all companies producing hoosiers. As efforts to modernize the kitchen continued, the hoosier inspired the concept of "streamlined" kitchen design, with built-in kitchen cupboards (wall and floor units with a continuous countertop). By the late 1930s the hoosier cabinet was no longer being produced.

Hanging spice box, pine, eleven drawers with porcelain knobs, 9½" wide × 16" tall, **$225.**

Chairs and Rockers

While the early settlers made do with crude benches and stools, it wasn't long before seating furniture took on great importance as both a necessity and a valuable form of expression and design.

Rockers, slat-back chairs and Windsor chairs were first made in America during the eighteenth century and the Hitchcock chair by 1818.

Certain types of chairs can be categorized as a regional style or design. For example, New England is noted for being the center of production of Windsors, the Boston rocker and Hitchcock chairs; many Sheraton fancy chairs were made in New York; and the Pennsylvania Dutch crafted numerous benches and sturdy chairs with folk art cutouts.

Most country chairs were crafted with a simplified interpretation of fash-

Rare fan-back Windsor slipper chair, eighteenth century, 16" wide × 34" tall, **$625.**

Fan-back Windsor chair, circa 1810–1820, inscribed "Adison Williams, East Weinhaur, Mass. Dec. 1913, Joseph Williams, this chair is now 100 years old," 17″ wide × 16″ deep × 34″ tall, **$795.**

Pine rod-back Windsor chair, 14″ wide × 14″ deep × 34″ tall, **$75.**

ionable city designs and were either quite plain or decorative. Traditional construction methods were employed until factory-made furniture became commonplace in the late nineteenth century.

The Windsor chair was first made in England and is named after the town of Windsor, where chairs were made and then shipped by boat to London retail centers. By the late 1700s the Windsor chair was being made in Philadelphia, New York City and urban areas throughout New England.

The earliest American-made Windsors had thick pine seats and backs crafted from hickory saplings. These early examples had finely crafted thin spindles, splayed legs and a saddle-shaped seat. They were often made

from a combination of woods and therefore most examples were painted, usually in a solid color.

Variations in style during the eighteenth century included the low-back and bow-back Windsors, and also the comb-back, fan-back and hoop-back Windsors. All were made with and without arms.

In his 1917 book *American Windsors*, author Wallace Nutting defines a Windsor as "a stick-leg chair, with a spindle back topped by a bent bow or comb. In a good Windsor, lightness, strength, grace, durability and quaintness are all found in an irresistible blend." Regarding the early craftsmanship of Windsors, Nutting tells us, "construction of the Windsor involves many delicate adjustments and

Ad from a 1910 Montgomery Ward "Grocery List."

On left, a nineteenth-century thumb-back Windsor chair, black with stenciled design, 14″ wide × 33″ tall, **$95;** on the right, an arrow-back plank chair, black with stenciled design, 14″ wide × 33″ tall, **$55.**

Thumb-back Windsor chair, green paint, 15″ wide × 14″ deep × 32″ tall, **$395.**

could only be made in fine form by specially trained men. For instance, the seat slants backward. The arm rail slants still more . . . spindles from center of back to last under the arm is bored at a different angle, and is slanted in two directions. The bow, when bored for the spindles is very much cut away and will break unless the best wood, carefully worked, is used.''

During the nineteenth century still more variations of the Windsor chair became popular as the basic design was altered to suit then-popular fashion and style. Examples include the rod-back (also called a birdcage Windsor), which sports Sheraton influence in the use of a top rail and a lower, parallel rail with decorative spindles in between (the rod-back design was employed once again during the early 1900s); arrow-back (as the name implies, spindles were constructed with an arrow shape); and the

A set of six children's chairs, painted either green or salmon, 12″ wide × 26″ tall, **$115 for all.**

Windsor thumb-back chairs with old red paint, circa 1875–1900, 15″ wide × 34″ tall, **$195.**

captain's chair, which became a popular form for office furniture and table seating. Windsor chairs for the kitchen were also popular and included rod-back, arrow-back and loop-back styles. As machines replaced craftsmen, the Windsor lost much of its detailing and factory-produced examples sported wider spindles and flat seats. In addition, the mid-nineteenth-century popularity of the country Victorian Sheraton Fancy chair

decreased the demand for hand-crafted Windsors. Factory-produced examples, however, continued to be made as the Windsor was recognized as a sturdy and functional form. For example, Windsor spindle-backs were incorporated into early twentieth century Colonial Revival (from 1880 to 1920, when early American designs were reproduced) furniture and can be seen in the massive amounts of oak seating pieces that were popular through the 1930s.

The Hitchcock chair was named after the man considered to be the father of the ornamental and stenciled chair, Lambert Hitchcock (1795–1852). Hitchcock established his first chair factory in Barkhamsted, Connecticut, in 1818. Barkhamsted's name was changed to Hitchcocksville in 1821 and the town's name was changed a third time in 1866 to Riverton.

Hitchcock's factory turned out fully assembled and decorated chairs geared toward middle-class Victorians

Half-spindle, plank seat chair, old red paint with gold trim, circa 1850, 16″ wide × 30″ tall, **$495 for set of eight.**

Sheraton fancy chair, circa 1820, original with the exception of rush seat, which was replaced in 1900, 17″ wide × 15″ deep × 33″ tall, **$65.**

Sheraton fancy chair, circa 1825, old rush seat, chair repainted around 1900, 17″ wide × 15″ deep × 33 ″ tall, **$65.**

(most of whom lived in rural areas). His chairs had birch or maple frames and rush seats, and later wooden or cane seats. Women and children were employed at the factory to paint and then stencil the chairs. By 1825 Hitchcock was turning out 15,000 chairs a year, and in 1826 he built a new and larger factory. His goods included a variety of different chairs, such as slat-backs, arrow-backs, Boston rockers and simple armchairs. In 1829 Hitchcock was forced into taking on a business partner due to his financial situation, and for the next fourteen years the company was known as Hitchcock, Alford and Company. He dissolved the partnership in 1843 and made an unsuccessful attempt to start another company.

Although many different nineteenth-century factories produced "Hitchcock" chairs, few labeled their

Slat-back kitchen chairs with original rush seats, painted blue, 16″ wide × 34″ tall, **$69 for the set.**

Slat-back armchair with rush seat, 21″ wide × 18″ deep × 41″ tall, **$195.**

Slat-back chair, painted white, 18″ wide × 43″ tall, **$195.**

Refinished pine Boston rocker, circa 1875–1899, 19″ wide × 18″ deep × 42″ tall, **$265.**

Maple arrow-back rocker, 20″ wide × 18″ deep × 40″ tall, **$145.**

goods. Hitchcock, however, made a practice of doing so and as a result, painted chairs with stenciled designs (often done in gold) are generically referred to as Hitchcock chairs. This often includes the Sheraton fancy painted chairs (with slat-backs), which early on were very formal in appearance and painted in light colors with hand-painted decorations. By 1820 stencils were being used to decorate these chairs, which were by then being painted in darker colors of black, brown, green, and pumpkin. Gold striping was commonplace.

By the mid-nineteenth century, chairs combining both Sheraton and Windsor influence became popular and the rush and cane seats on Sheraton fancy chairs gave way to plank seats. (However, production of chairs with rush or cane seats started up once again

in the early 1900s.) Imitative graining was more popular than painted decorations and striping was often done with colors rather than gold.

Slat-back (also known as ladder-back) chairs were first made in England and were being crafted in America by the 1690s. The slat-back is comprised of a simple design with horizontal slats that country furniture craftsmen found appealing. Early examples of this chair were made with rush seats (splint was later used and Shaker examples used colored tape), had four or five slats across their high back, and frequently were painted. Some slat-backs also had fancy touches such as turned posts, but by the late 1700s the trend was toward the plain and simple, which resulted in slat-backs often being made with only two or three slats. Many examples from the nineteenth century have only two

Child's pine rocker, circa 1850, 11½" wide ×
20" tall, **$55.**

Child's slat-back rocker, mid–nineteenth century, traces of old red paint, 12" wide × 10" deep
× 20" tall, **$150.**

Early comb-back Windsor rocker, **$700–$1000;**
bracket-foot blanket chest, dovetailed construction, **$600–$800.** Photo courtesy of *AntiqueWeek.*

Oak lady's rocker with fabric seat and back, 17"
wide × 37" tall, **$95.**

Tiger maple child's rocker with carpet seat and back, 12″ wide × 12″ deep × 24″ tall, **$275.**

Pine rocker, 18″ wide × 14″ deep × 32″ tall, **$295.**

slats while others have more. For example, slat-backs produced by the Shakers continued to be constructed with three, four and five slats through the early 1900s.

Some slat-back design and construction can be attributed to a certain area of the country based on the shape of the slats used in the chair. For example, those slat-backs crafted in New England usually have straight slats and posts while a chair made in Pennsylvania often has curved slats. French Canadian slat-backs have curved slats and arms.

Slat-backs were constructed of a variety of woods, including cherry, oak, chestnut, walnut, maple, birch, poplar, hickory and pine, and were constructed with mortise and tenon joints until the nineteenth century when nails were used in chair construction. The slat-back design remained popular and influenced the production of many Shera-

Child's Boston Rocker, black with gold and red stencils, 12″ wide × 15″ tall, **$125.**

ton fancy chairs and Mission oak chairs turned out during the early 1900s.

Probably one of the most classic examples of American country furniture, the rocking chair hails from the mid-eighteenth century when rockers were attached to a slat-back chair. These rockers, or curved pieces of wood, were attached to chairs by way of a groove cut into the bottom of the chair leg or by either pegging or bolting the rocker to the outside of the leg. Earliest examples had rockers which were of equal distance beyond both front and back legs, but by the early 1800s the back rocker was longer.

During the early nineteenth century, the Hitchcock chair factory produced Windsor-style rocking chairs, available with a grain-painted or colored finish; the Shaker communities were turning out slat-back rocking chairs; and the well-known Boston rocker was designed and reportedly first manufactured in the city of Boston.

The Boston rocker was characterized by a rolled seat, curled arms (or no arms), and a backing of spindles with a

Youth chair and walker ad from 1924 Montgomery Ward catalog.

Hints on Chairs and Rockers

Inspect chairs for obvious signs of age, such as worn rungs and stretchers.

Examine the leg joints and underneath chair seats on painted pieces to determine an original or old painted finish.

Keep in mind that older slat-back chairs will have more slats than nineteenth-century examples and reproductions do not exhibit the quality craftsmanship, construction or normal signs of wear you would expect to find on an authentic country piece.

To help determine age on rockers, remember to inspect the rockers. The longer the rear rocker, the later the piece was made.

Doll's oak highchair with Dutch boy and girl design, circa 1930s, 11″ wide × 9″ deep × 29″ tall, **$30.**

Pine highchair, 11½″ wide × 34½″ tall, **$125.**

wide top slat which was stenciled with flowers, landscape scenes, bowls or baskets of fruit, or other designs.

A variety of early rockers were constructed of softwood for the seat and hardwoods (hickory, ash, oak and maple) for the legs, arms, stretchers and spindles. From the 1850s on, many rockers were being factory made, constructed entirely of maple, and left with a natural wood finish.

While the rocker was quick to excite Americans, who embraced it and eagerly took it into their homes, it caused quite a stir among Europeans who were skeptical of such "rocking." For example, the 1960 publication of *The Ornamented Chair* includes a number of articles by various authors. In an excerpt from Harriet Martineau's 1838 article entitled "Retrospect of Western Travel," she reported, "in these small inns (between Stockbridge, Massachusetts and Albany, New York) the disagreeable practice of rocking in the chair is seen in its excess. In the Inn parlors are three or four rocking chairs in which sit ladies who are vibrating in different directions and at various velocities, so as to try the head of a stranger. . . . How this lazy and ungraceful indulgence ever became general, I cannot imagine; but the nation seems so wedded to it, that I see little chance of its being forsaken."

Chests and Chests of Drawers

When the colonists made the journey to America, their clothing, a few precious valuables and papers, and perhaps a few small household goods were safely packed in a wooden chest. Even in the first hastily constructed one-room house, this chest would serve several purposes. It was not only for storage, but also served as a table or for seating.

During the seventeenth century the six-board chest was most popular. As the name implies, the six-board chest was simply constructed of six wooden planks: the bottom board, two side pieces (which also served as feet), front and back boards, and a lid.

By the eighteenth century, European trends influenced skilled American craftsmen to make chests with a single drawer below. This design was expanded upon, especially in urban areas, and the results were the chest on chest and the highboy.

Highboys, which were especially popular during the eighteenth century, were constructed in two pieces. The bottom pieces have tall legs and the top resembles a chest of drawers.

Pine six-board footed blanket chest, circa 1870, green wash, 37″ wide × 19½″ deep × 24″ tall, **$485.**

Pine blanket box, dovetailed base, mustard paint, 65″ long, 23½″ wide × 28″ tall, **$375.**

Seven-board pine blanket chest made in Pennsylvania, circa 1860, feather grain painted, bunn feet, dovetailed, all original, 48″ long × 21½″ deep × 23½″ tall, **$950.**

Doll's factory-made chest of drawers, dovetailed construction, 15″ wide × 9″ deep × 16″ tall, **$150.**

Pine lift-top blanket chest with two drawers, 43″ wide × 18″ deep × 40″ tall, **$625.**

Blanket box, framed construction with panel inserts, **$400–$600.** Photo courtesy of *AntiqueWeek.*

Four-drawer cherry bonnet chest with wooden pulls, **$900–$1200.** Photo courtesy of *AntiqueWeek.*

Five-drawer tiger maple bonnet chest, glass knobs, scalloped skirt, especially fine piece, **$1000–$1400.** Photo courtesy of *AntiqueWeek.*

One-piece bureau bookcase with three drawers and leaded glass inserts in cupboard doors, scalloped skirt, popular piece for a child's room, **$800–$1000.** Photo courtesy of *AntiqueWeek.*

Four-drawer bonnet chest, tiger maple inlays above columns, **$1100–$1500.** Photo courtesy of *AntiqueWeek.*

Pine trunk in original, excellent condition, rounded corners, 30″ wide × 18″ deep × 17″ tall, **$450.**

Jenny Lind pine trunk, 25″ long × 15″ deep × 14″ tall, **$175.**

Large dome-top trunk, fancy and decorative, 38″ wide × 22″ deep × 28″ tall, **$325.**

Flat-top trunk, 36″ wide × 22″ deep × 24″ tall, **$39.**

Flat-top trunk with rounded corners, 36″ wide × 22″ deep × 25″ tall, **$59.**

Dome-top trunk, 36" wide × 21" deep × 30½" tall, **$88.**

A chest-on-chest, while similar to the highboy, is actually two chests, one on top of the other, and does not have the tall legs characteristically found on the highboy.

Another case piece, the tall chest of drawers, was in vogue from the mid-eighteenth century on and is of one-piece construction with little or no ornamentation. Tall chests of drawers continued to be made well into the twentieth century when oak furniture factories, Colonial Revival furniture manufacturers and followers of the Mission style turned out five- and six-drawer chests in a variety of sizes.

The six-board chest (or blanket chest as it is best known) remained popular throughout the centuries and continued to be made in rural areas during the 1800s. Much like early examples, many were constructed with feet made from the two end planks while others sat right on the floor. Blanket chests were usually painted, grained or decorated with hand-painted designs. (See the Introduction for information on Pennsylvania Dutch dower chests.)

The most common chest construction is categorized as "boarded." This method is used in the six-board chest, where the planks are dovetailed together (in early examples), pegged, or nailed. Other chests were crafted by attaching planks to a corner post or by framing a chest and using paneled inserts.

During the late nineteenth century another type of chest became popular mainly for travel but also for storage. Factory-produced trunks were available in a wide variety of sizes and styles for both men and women and could be purchased through the popular mail-order catalogs. The 1895 Montgomery Ward and Company catalog offered more than forty different trunks, including dome-lids, flat tops and

Three-drawer pine chest, 40″ wide × 32″ tall, **$325.**

Four-drawer dresser, dovetailed construction, brown paint, 39″ wide × 17½″ deep × 35″ tall, **$195.**

Three-drawer chest with newer paint and stenciling, original bunn feet, Pennsylvania-Dutch origin, circa 1830, 37″ wide × 16″ deep × 35″ tall, **$295.**

Chestnut three-drawer dresser with carved walnut pulls, 39″ wide × 16½″ deep × 36″ tall, **$525.**

Pine chest of drawers, 43″ wide × 21″ deep × 45″ tall, **$395.**

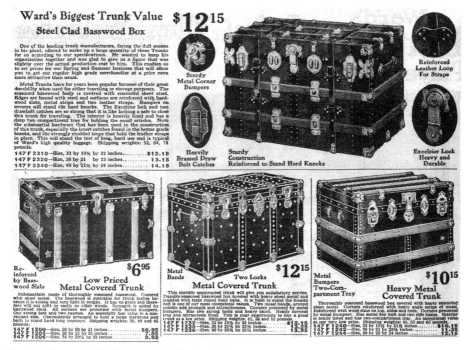

Trunk ad from a 1924 Montgomery Ward catalog.

Ward's Biggest Trunk Value
Steel Clad Basswood Box
$12¹⁵

One of the leading trunk manufacturers, facing the dull season in his plant, offered to make up a large quantity of these Trunks for us according to our specifications. He wanted to keep his organization together and was glad to give us a figure that was slightly over the actual production cost to him. This enables us to set prices for our Spring and Summer business that will allow you to get our regular high grade merchandise at a price even more attractive than usual.

Metal Trunks have for years been popular because of their great durability when used for either traveling or storage purposes. The seasoned basswood body is covered with enameled sheet steel. Edges are bound with steel and surfaces are reinforced with hardwood slats, metal strips and two leather straps. Bumpers on corners will stand the hard knocks. The Excelsior lock and two drawbolt catches are so strong that it is like locking a safe to close this trunk for traveling. The interior is heavily lined and has a deep two compartment tray for holding the small articles. Note the substantial hardware that has been used in the construction of this trunk, especially the latest catches found in the better grade trunks, and the strongly studded loops that hold the leather straps in place. This will stand the test of long, hard use and is typical of Ward's high quality luggage. Shipping weights: 52, 64, 71 pounds.

147 F 2310—Size, 32 by 19½ by 22 inches.......... $12.15
147 F 2320—Size, 36 by 21 by 23 inches.......... 13.15
147 F 2340—Size, 40 by 21½ by 24 inches.......... 14.15

Sturdy Metal Corner Bumpers

Heavily Brassed Draw Bolt Catches

Sturdy Construction Reinforced to Stand Hard Knocks

Reinforced Leather Loop For Straps

Excelsior Lock Heavy and Durable

Reinforced by Basswood Slats

$6⁹⁵
Low Priced Metal Covered Trunk

Substantially made of thoroughly seasoned basswood. Covered with sheet metal. The basswood is desirable for trunk bodies because it is strong and very light in weight. It has no grain and therefore will not split as easily as other woods. Strength is added by hardwood slats. All corners are protected with metal bumpers. One strong lock and two catches. An especially fine value in a convenient size. Conveniently arranged to hold a large wardrobe and built to stand hard long journeys. Shipping weights: 36, 40 and 45 pounds.

147 F 1200—Size, 26 by 20 by 21 inches............ $6.95
147 F 1204—Size, 36 by 21 by 22 inches............ 7.85
147 F 1206—Size, 34 by 20½ by 23 inches............ 8.85

Metal Bands

$12¹⁵
Two Locks
Metal Covered Trunk

This sturdily constructed trunk will give you satisfactory service. Durable seasoned basswood box covered with heavy sheet metal and studded with large round head nails. It is built to stand the knocks and is one of our most exceptional values. Two metal bands around outside add strength and attractiveness. Corners protected by metal bumpers. Has two strong locks and heavy catch. Neatly covered tray and attractively lined. This is your opportunity to buy a good trunk at a low price. Shipping weights: 45, 50 and 55 pounds.

147 F 1232—Size, 32 by 19½ by 22 inches............ $12.15
147 F 1234—Size, 36 by 21¼ by 23½ inches............ 13.15
147 F 1236—Size, 40 by 21½ by 23½ inches............ 13.95

Metal Bumpers Two-Compartment Tray

$10¹⁵
Heavy Metal Covered Trunk

Thoroughly seasoned basswood box covered with heavy enameled sheet metal. Corners reinforced with heavy angle strips of metal. Reinforced with wood slats on top, sides and ends. Corners protected by metal bumpers. Has metal key lock and two side hasps. Interior is neatly lined and has two-compartment tray. An exceptional value at our very low price. Shipping weights: 45, 53 and 65 pounds.

147 F 1240—Size, 32 by 19½ by 21½ inches............ $10.15
147 F 1242—Size, 36 by 21 by 23½ inches............ 11.35
147 F 1244—Size, 40 by 22 by 24 inches............ 12.15

Hints on Chests and Chests of Drawers

Dower chests were made until the mid-nineteenth century; few were made after that. Today they are rare and costly. Examine them carefully for authenticity of both the chest and the finish.

Six-board chests or blanket chests are still available for collecting. Check construction methods and hardware, look for signs of age and wear, and examine a painted finish carefully.

Check construction methods on four-drawer chests—hardware and knobs, tool marks and other features—to determine age.

straight-back wall trunks. These travel trunks (or steamer trunks, as they are known) were plain or ornate, with a zinc, leather or canvas covering, wooden slats, iron or brass hardware; and leather straps. They varied in price from 50 cents for a small, 24-inch round-top trunk with imitation leather to $18 for a 36-inch "Ladies Special Leather Bound Brass Trimmed Trunk." This particular trunk was advertised as "made of selected basswood, covered with heavy canvas and painted; barrel top, long hardwood slats . . . stitched leather handles; slats, corners and valance protected by brass clamps . . . tray with bonnet box, portfolio in top, clothlined throughout, extra dress tray."

From storage or blanket chests came the chest of drawers. During the nineteenth century many different country pieces were made, both by hand and then later by machine. The four-drawer chest was common, and after 1850 these were constructed mainly of pine and often painted or given an imitation grain finish.

Tables and Desks

Several different types of country tables were crafted and used during the nineteenth century. The majority were made from pine, walnut, maple, and cherry or a combination of woods, with pine usually used for the table top.

Drop-leaf tables generally have hardware underneath to hold a leaf in place, while gate-leg tables have a leg which will swing out to support the leaf. Both gate-leg and drop-leaf tables were popular during the 1800s because of their space-saving feature. They were made in assorted shapes with rectangu-

Cherry drop-leaf table, 36″ long × 40″ wide, **$440.**

Maple drop-leaf table, 45½″ long × 48″ wide with leaves up, **price not available.**

Maple drop-leaf table with scalloped edges, old red paint, 34″ long × 33″ wide with leaves up, **$525.**

lar, oval or round table tops. While drop-leaf tables characteristically have straight or spool-turned legs, gate-legs have turnings (which were simplified during the nineteenth century.)

Larger tables of sturdy construction include the farmhouse table, a long table of six to eight feet in length with scrubbed pine top and hardwood legs; the harvest table, with a long narrow top (usually pine) and a drop-leaf on either side so the table size could be increased; and the sawbuck table with its five-to-six-foot table top supported by criss-crossed legs at either end. The sawbuck table also typically was made of pine or had a pine top with hardwood legs.

Tavern tables were used extensively during the 1700s and were crafted with

Pine and walnut farm table, 72″ long × 30″ wide, **$300.**

Pine farm table, 84″ long × 30″ wide, **$550.**

different regional characteristics, but most were intended for use by the patrons in local taverns and were similarly designed and constructed with stretchers bracing the legs together. Examples from the nineteenth century are simplified versions of older examples and are generally five feet long and up to 35 inches wide with stretchers, plain skirting and no drawers. Tavern tables were often constructed from a combination of woods and most were painted.

Trestle tables were in use for centuries (and can be traced back to the Middle Ages), but their design remained basically the same: a one-board

Old pine table with breadboard top, traces of old blue paint, 36″ long × 23″ wide × 30″ tall, **$250.**

Kitchen table, unusual with a dovetailed front, splayed legs, two-board top, 48″ long × 22¼″ wide × 32″ tall, **$185.**

Pine farm table, note fancy legs, 84″ long × 32″ wide, **$550.**

Small pine and cherry table with tapered legs, 16″ wide × 28″ tall, **$150.**

Kitchen worktable, maple and poplar, original drawer pulls, circa 1880, 45″ long × 24″ deep × 30″ tall, **$595.**

Round pine candlestand, 12″ across × 28″ tall, **$115.**

Small butternut worktable, one drawer, nice detail on legs, 18″ wide × 19″ deep × 28″ tall, **$275.**

Cherry one-drawer stand, 18″ wide × 28″ tall, **$250.**

Rare Mt. Lebanon Shaker infirmary candlestand, 14″ wide × 14″ deep × 26″ tall, **$2650.**

top whose "trestles" were strengthened by use of a stretcher. During the nineteenth century the Shakers adapted the trestle table for their own use.

Work-related kitchen tables include the baker's table, which has one or two large possum-belly bins for flour and meal, and a scrubbed-pine (later zinc and then porcelain enamel) top for preparing baked goods and meals. Chopping tables were also popular and, as their name implies, were used for preparing foods for cooking. Both types of tables were constructed of pine or maple and sometimes oak.

Candlestands with a small square,

Shaker table-top desk, 17″ wide × 15″ deep × 12″ tall, **$950.**

Pine slant-front desk, inside is a small drawer with an unusual hidden compartment, 26″ wide × 21″ deep × 36″ tall, **$425.**

Two-piece cherry desk, circa 1820–1835, made in New York, cupboard over desk is very unusual, 39″ wide × 22″ deep × 75″ tall, **$2450.**

Pine school desk, 22″ long × 24″ wide × 40″ tall, **$325.**

Cherry drop-lid desk, sold at auction for **$300;** cherry pedestal table, sold at auction for **$280.** Photo courtesy of *AntiqueWeek.*

Pine desk, circa 1840, square peg construction, tapered legs, 30″ wide × 27″ deep × 31″ tall, **$350.**

Cherry drop-front secretary desk with spool-turned decorations in door panels, **$800–$1200.** Photo courtesy of *AntiqueWeek.*

Country davenport desk, **$400–$600.** Photo courtesy of *AntiqueWeek.*

Cherry and tiger maple one-drawer stand, sold at auction for **$3700.** Photo courtesy of *AntiqueWeek.*

Small pine one-drawer table, **$300–$500.** Photo courtesy of *AntiqueWeek.*

Early slant-top desk, small in size, **$400–$600.** Photo courtesy of *AntiqueWeek.*

Examine tables for style, consistency in construction, uniform patina, expected wear marks, and scrubbed tops. If painted, inspect joints for any signs of new or touched-up paint. Beware of reproductions and pieces made from old parts.

With desks, look out for "married" pieces—tables and bookcases combined and presented as secretary desks. When inspecting such pieces, visually consider "style." If your initial impression is that the top and bottom don't belong together, you've probably stumbled across a married piece.

Inspect any painted table or desk for an authentic or old finish. Since a large country desk with a drawer or multiple pigeonholes is a very popular piece, check for evidence of newly cut wood, joints, and any other parts to be certain they haven't been added to increase the value of an old piece.

round, rectangular or oval top (some were tilt-tops) resting on a tripod or pillar base were popular during the eighteenth and nineteenth centuries. They were first used to set candles on and later lamps.

The earliest desks were lap-top boxes, first with a flat top and later a slanted lid, in which the first settlers stored their important papers and the family Bible or prayer book. By the early eighteenth century this portable wooden box had become a stationary piece of furniture with a fall-front. Before long a top piece was added with shelving and an assortment of little cubbyholes for storage. This top section evolved into a glass-enclosed bookcase creating the secretary. By the early 1800s a more common country piece called the secretary desk was being crafted from maple, cherry or mahogany and was actually a one-drawer table with a narrow top piece (set back) with bookshelves behind blind-front cupboard doors.

Several other types of desks came into being in the nineteenth century, including fall-front and drop-lid desks

Child's oak chalkboard with easel and roll-pictures at top, 22″ wide × 46″ tall, **$95.**

that resembled chests of drawers and multipurpose slant-front desks that were simply constructed of whatever wood was readily available and often painted a red, brown or blue.

Collectors also come across large country desks used during the 1800s as a schoolmaster's desk or as a desk in the general store or office. These tall desks have plain-board sides and skirt, are made of pine (many with hardwood legs), are constructed with dovetail joints or nailed together, and often painted. A schoolmaster's desk often had a long drawer, and desks built for use in a store or office frequently had dividers and/or pigeonholes underneath their lift-top lid.

Dry Sinks, Benches and Stools

During the nineteenth century a variety of utilitarian pieces were used for stacking, storing, washing and seating. Most were very simple in design and hastily crafted to serve an immediate need.

From the early 1800s through the turn of the century, dry sinks were constructed across the vast rural areas to serve as sinks or washtubs. The first dry sinks were no more than rudimentary bucket benches with troughlike enclosures on top to hold water. As the dry sink developed, the bottom was en- closed and it gained cupboard doors. These low, cupboardlike dry sinks were found in the kitchen where the zinc-lined sink could be filled from the hand pump or from water-filled buckets that stood by on the back porch.

Most dry sinks were constructed with nails, made of pine or a combination of softwoods, and often painted. Common colors for painting a dry sink included green, red, blue, yellow and gray, and the cupboard door(s) either had wooden or porcelain knobs or brass pulls. Wooden latches were most com-

Cherry Ohio Amish two-drawer dry sink in mustard grain-painted decoration, 42″ wide, sold at auction for **$900**. Photo courtesy of *AntiqueWeek*.

Dry sink, New York State origin, circa 1840, old salmon paint, 30″ wide × 20″ deep × 31″ tall, **$1225.**

Pine dry sink, 50″ wide × 21″ deep × 32″ tall, **$1150.**

Pine bucket bench with traces of original red paint, 25″ wide × 12″ deep × 30″ tall, **$795.**

Pine dry sink, 38″ wide × 20″ deep × 34″ tall, **$495.**

Pine bucket bench with old salmon color paint, 30″ wide × 10½″ deep × 30″ tall, **$215.**

Shaker bucket bench with one drawer, 45″ wide × 20″ deep × 33″ tall, **$2500.**

Pine bucket bench, 27″ wide × 24″ tall, **$525.**

Three-tier pine plant/vegetable stand, painted white, 34″ wide at the bottom × 36″ tall, **$95.**

Oak church pew, 60″ long × 36″ tall, **$395.**

Stepstool, green with traces of old blue paint, 14″ across × 10″ tall, **35.**

Railroad station stepstool, old blue milk paint, 15½″ wide × 10″ tall, **$55.**

Hints on Dry Sinks, Benches and Stools

Dry sinks have long been favorites among country collectors, and reproductions have been turning up to meet the demand. Take your time when examining a dry sink; inspect construction, style and finish carefully. Be sure to ask questions of the dealer and have him indicate on your receipt whether or not the piece is authentic.

Pine footstool, recent blue paint, 15″ across × 10″ tall, **$15.**

Printer's stool, 14″ wide × 28″ tall, **$95.**

mon, but some examples may have an iron latch.

While the dry sink served an important purpose in the country kitchen, a bucket bench was still needed on the back porch to store the assortment of water pitchers, dippers, soap, laundry supplies, and other sundries well into the late 1800s. Heavy water-filled buckets were stored on the bottom shelf.

Most bucket benches are of open-shelf construction, but some were crafted with a cupboard door and some-

times a drawer, and most were made of pine (although maple and cherry examples have been found). They were often painted.

Seating benches were commonplace during the nineteenth century, mainly for use at the long kitchen table.

Semicircular stepped shelves were used during the late 1800s for selling produce or displaying plants. These were usually painted green.

Early on, footstools were found by the fireplace. These small stools were crafted of pine and were no more than eight inches tall. Some examples are very crude—with four legs stuck into a plank top; others have plain or decorative sides.

Other stools, such as the taller splayed-leg stools, were made for chores such as milking the cow. During the long-running heyday of the railroad, low stepstools were found at every train station. These had a rectangular opening in the top so the stool could easily be picked up and moved.

Today, along with assorted country benches and stools, collectors also snap up old wooden church pews.

French-Canadian Furniture

No discussion of country furniture would be complete without mentioning the abundance of French-Canadian country pieces that have made their way into the United States over the past sixty years.

Nineteenth-century Quebec farmers and unskilled craftsmen created simple, sturdy furniture pieces in time-honored ways to fill a variety of needs. The post-and-frame construction method had been practiced by the French in Quebec since the 1600s, and this method of joinery continued through the 1800s.

Most French-Canadian pieces (especially cupboards and armoires) were crafted from white pine and butternut

Large French-Canadian pine four-door cupboard, old blue-green paint, 51″ wide × 19″ deep × 76″ tall, **$2200.**

French-Canadian folk art hanging cupboard, old yellow with green paint, 17″ wide × 27″ tall, **$375.**

French-Canadian pine rocker, pegged construction, circa 1860, traces of old red paint, original seat, 20″ wide × 14″ deep × 32″ tall, **$245.**

French-Canadian country chair, snowshoe woven seat, old light blue paint, 15″ wide × 13″ deep × 34″ tall, **$185.**

Canadian country armchair from Nova Scotia, circa 1850, blue paint has been restored, 22″ wide × 18″ deep × 32″ tall, **$145.**

during the early 1800s. Later, white ash, birch and maple were also used in furniture construction.

French-Canadian cupboards, chairs, washstands and tables were often painted dark blue, light blue, brick red, mustard and olive green.

Pieces such as cupboards and armoires tend to be quite large; tables and chairs are often very low; moldings, scrolled aprons, and skirts often were used as a decorative touch; rockers and cradles are often recognized by the exceptionally large rockers (three-to-four inches thick); and many "habitant," or country, chairs exhibit mortise and tenon construction with a seat woven of rush, bark strips, rawhide (in a snowshoe weave), twisted yarn or thick twine. Often times an old French newspaper was used as a lining in case pieces

General Hints

Regardless of what country furniture piece you are looking at or considering to buy, keep in mind that prices have risen as a direct result of country furniture's popularity and the scarcity of certain pieces. Therefore, be suspicious of any deal that seems too good to be true. Obviously underpriced or suspicious-looking country furniture may be constructed from old parts—a "reworked" piece that has been altered in some way to meet current demands (adding carvings, drawers, shortening legs, shaving height); a "married" piece in which two parts are joined to appear as one original unit; or a misrepresented reproduction.

What about the country furniture piece that has been repaired or had its hardware replaced? It would be foolish to think all furniture can survive year after working year without sustaining some injury to the finish/construction, broken/missing hardware, or just the effects of time. Restoration is certainly acceptable provided it is done as accurately as possible and preferably by a professional. For example, the feet on cupboards, chests, and other pieces often require repair, replacement or removal due to damage caused by water, insects, rodents, and time.

Small Canadian pine table with scalloped bottom shelf, 23″ wide × 19″ deep × 28″ tall, **$245.**

French-Canadian table from Quebec, old red paint, 24″ wide × 18″ deep × 26″ tall, **$575.**

and may be discovered in drawers and under shelves.

While many pieces made in Quebec were strictly of French-Canadian origin, other pieces display multicultural influence that resulted from increased contact with the Americans and British during the nineteenth century.

Collectors should note that French-Canadian country furniture is very beautiful and is sometimes mis-

Folk art stand, circa 1900, burntwood or "Flemish Art" design and painted, 12″ wide × 15″ tall, **$140.**

taken for Pennsylvania-Dutch furniture. Collectors also should be aware that enough French-Canadian furniture has made its way across the border into the United States to warrant becoming familiar with its style and characteristics in order to recognize it and better appreciate it. The height of this furniture migration occurred during the 1950s and 1960s, when antiques "pickers" and "haulers" carted it by the truckful from rural Quebec into the neighboring border states of Vermont, New Hampshire and New York. From there, French-Canadian country furniture has made its way all across the country.

SECTION IV
Country Furniture Additions

In the February 1881 issue of *Lippincott's Magazine*, an article entitled "A Country Tavern in Winter," written by Mary Dean, related the ambience of a country inn.

Two o'clock by the kitchen clock. At four it will be dark . . . the tavern stands knee-deep in snow . . . nevertheless, "flowers of all heavens" grow in the landlady's windows. A large, dark, able woman, she sews beside her flowers, half remembering the brief dream of summer. . . . She has made a sitting-room of her ample old kitchen, has fitted it up with a rag carpet, a cherry bureau inlaid with birch and a stand having gorgeous brass handles and a pair of green-glass candlesticks, and has moved her kitchen, according to a fashion dear to country wives, back to a little pantry-surrounded room in the rear. . . . She can look across the yellow-painted dining room to a door of the bar-room, which opens occasionally with the announcement "Two travellers for dinner!" Whenever this happens, the little pot standing full of peeled potatoes in cold water in the kitchen is clapped on the fire and twenty minutes later, those potatoes, mashed, enter the dining room in the company of ham and eggs and hot coffee. There are long, level roads where the railroads have killed the taverns but among the hills a great deal of riding and driving still goes on . . . and many a traveller breasts the storm miles and miles for the sake of the landlady's cookery.

These words written well over 100 years ago offer a subtle reflection of the changes taking place during the nineteenth century. The growing Industrial Revolution brought with it improved transportation—first through the canals, then railroads, and finally the automobile.

Well over 3000 miles of canals were built between 1817 and 1840, including the Erie Canal, which escorted both immigrants with their craft skills, and later, modernization into Middle America.

From 1840 to the turn of the century, railroads were built all across the country and furniture factories, textile mills and small shops sprang up in the shadow of railroad stations to assure continuous shipment of their goods and products. Prior to 1850 furniture manufacturing was concentrated along the East Coast, but with the rapid spread of railroad transportation, this growing industry soon covered the country. In fact, industry as a whole grew at such a fast pace that by the second half of the nineteenth century the United States was being recognized as an industrial giant by the rest of the world.

The Introduction of Mail-Order Catalogs

The Industrial Revolution brought about changes in lifestyle, both for city dwellers and for the farmer whose workday was somewhat shortened by new technology. Country living no longer meant everything had to be crafted by hand; mail-order shopping brought the latest style and fashion right to the farmer's front door. Along with furnishings this included everything from canned foods and medicinal remedies to furniture, linens and clothing.

Large furniture factories, many of which were located throughout the East and Midwest (especially in Grand Rapids, Michigan) were able to turn out large quantities of machine-made furniture pieces thanks to new high-speed precision saws. These furnishings became extremely popular with middle-class Americans who found them to be affordable, stylish and easily delivered by way of catalogs.

Montgomery Ward and Company

The first and one of the largest catalogs to emerge during the late 1800s was that of Montgomery Ward and Company. Aaron Montgomery Ward founded his mail-order business in 1872 and chose Chicago as his base of operations. Ward had worked both as a traveling salesman and as the manager of a general store, so he was well aware of the needs of the rural population. By buying in bulk from manufacturers and

Dining sets available through the 1924 Montgomery Ward catalog.

In 1925 this full-page ad in a popular woman's magazine promoted mail-order fashions and cost savings via the Montgomery Ward catalog.

selling directly to the farmers via his catalog, Ward was able to offer very low prices on his goods. What began as a one-page flyer soon became a booklet, and by the early 1880s the Montgomery Ward and Company catalog was 240 pages full of almost 10,000 different items illustrated with woodcuts (a method of printing drawings). By the 1890s Ward's business had become so large that catalogs were over 500 pages long. The company proclaimed, "our mail-order business is the largest in the United States."

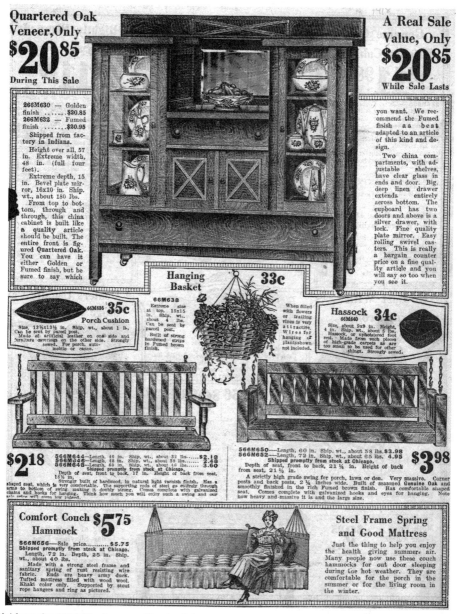

Quartered Oak Veneer, Only $20⁸⁵ During This Sale

A Real Sale Value, Only $20⁸⁵ While Sale Lasts

266M630 — Golden finish $20.85
266M632 — Fumed finish $20.95
Shipped from factory in Indiana.
Height over all, 57 in. Extreme width, 48 in. (full four feet).
Extreme depth, 15 in. Bevel plate mirror, 16x10 in. Ship. wt., about 180 lbs.
From top to bottom, through and through, this china cabinet is built like a quality article should be built. The entire front is figured Quartered Oak. You can have it either Golden or Fumed finish, but be sure to say which

you want. We recommend the Fumed finish as best adapted to an article of this kind and design.
Two china compartments, with adjustable shelves, have clear glass in ends and door. Big, deep linen drawer extends entirely across bottom. The cupboard has two doors and above is a silver drawer, with lock. Fine quality plate mirror. Easy rolling swivel casters. This is really a bargain counter price on a fine quality article and you will say so too when you see it.

Hanging Basket 33c
66M638
Extreme size at top, 15x15 in. Ship. wt., about 4 lbs.
Can be sent by parcel post.
Built of strong hardwood strips in Fumed brown finish.
When filled with flowers or trailing vines is very attractive. Wires for hanging of plants shown not included.

66M636 35c Porch Cushion
Size, 13½x13½ in. Ship. wt., about 1 lb.
Can be sent by parcel post.
Made of artificial leather on one side and furniture covering on the other side. Strongly sewed. For porch, automobile or canoe.

Hassock 34c
66M640
Size, about 9x9 in. Height, 4 in. Ship. wt., about 5 lbs.
Hassock, or upholstered foot rest. Made from such pieces of high-grade carpets as are too small to be used for other things. Strongly sewed.

$2¹⁸
566M644—Length, 40 in. Ship. wt., about 32 lbs...$2.18
566M646—Length, 48 in. Ship. wt., about 38 lbs....2.48
566M648—Length, 60 in. Ship. wt., about 46 lbs....3.60
Shipped promptly from stock at Chicago.
Depth of seat, front to back, 17 in. Height of back from seat, 18½ in.
Strongly built of hardwood, in natural light varnish finish. Has a shaped seat, which is very comfortable. The supporting rods of steel go entirely through arms to bottom of swing making it doubly strong. Comes complete with galvanized chains and hooks for hanging. Think how much you will enjoy such a swing and our

$3⁹⁸
566M650—Length, 60 in. Ship. wt., about 58 lbs.$3.98
566M652—Length, 72 in. Ship. wt., about 65 lbs. 4.95
Shipped promptly from stock at Chicago.
Depth of seat, front to back, 21½ in. Height of back from seat, 21½ in.
A strictly high grade swing for porch, lawn or den. Very massive. Corner posts and back posts, 2¼ inches wide. Built of seasoned Genuine Oak and smoothly finished in the rich Fumed brown finish. Has comfortable shaped seat. Comes complete with galvanized hooks and eyes for hanging. Note how heavy and massive it is and the large size.

Comfort Couch Hammock $5⁷⁵
566M656—Sale price...........$5.75
Shipped promptly from stock at Chicago.
Length, 72 in. Depth, 25 in. Ship. wt., about 40 lbs.
Made with a strong steel frame and sanitary spring of rust resisting wire fabric. Ends are heavy army duck. Tufted mattress filled with wood wool. Khaki color only. Supported by stout rope hangers and ring as pictured.

Steel Frame Spring and Good Mattress
Just the thing to help you enjoy the health giving summer air. Many people now use these couch hammocks for out door sleeping during the hot weather. They are comfortable for the porch in the summer or for the living room in the winter.

Ad from the 1918 Montgomery Ward catalog.

While the typical 1890s catalog included 38 different departments, more pages were allocated to more popular sellers, and furniture was one of them. Other big sellers included guns and sporting goods, hardware, watches and jewelry, clothing, books, dry goods, harnesses and saddles, tinware and cutlery, and crockery and glassware.

In the Montgomery Ward and Company spring and summer 1895 catalog, opening remarks told readers,

108

Solid Oak

A beautiful, Genuine San Luis Design Mission Set of six pieces. Strongly built of genuine Oak. This Set will please every member of your household, not only for its comfort giving qualities but for the distinctive tone which it will lend to your home. Nothing quite equals mission for that simple charm so much appreciated by every one. The seats are covered with Brown Imitation Spanish Leather. The set is decorated with beautiful scrolled panels. Finished a rich fumed brown. Wide arm rests on chair and rocker add greatly to their comfort. Shipped taken apart to save you freight.

Table. Top is 34 inches long by 23 inches wide. The posts are 1¾ inches square. Large lower shelf for magazines and books. Attractive scrolled panels in each end.

Arm Chair and Arm Rocker. Very comfortable. Seats are upholstered with Imitation Spanish Leather. Scrolled panels in back. Seats, 19 by 18 inches. Height of back from seat, 22½ inches.

Tabouret. A plant or flowers always appear more attractive when nicely displayed. This pretty tabouret will serve a very decorative purpose in your library, or living room by showing a fern or flowers to the best advantage. Top, 10 inches in diameter. Height, 17 inches.

Side Chair and Rocker. A comfortable, full size chair and rocker. Seats are 15 by 14 inches. Height of backs from seats, 20 inches.

166 F 544—6-Piece Set. Shipping weight, about 165 lbs........$22.95
166 F 545—Table only. Ship. weight, about 65 lbs.......$7.75

Master-Made Mission Furniture

TRADE MARK

$22⁹⁵

Complete
6-Piece
Set

Montgomery Ward covered all stylistic bases, including Mission furniture.

Our business was organized in 1872 to meet the wants of the Patrons of Husbandry, from whom we then received our main support. We did not, however, refuse the patronage of any person, knowing that the more goods we handled the cheaper we could sell them. . . . We do not wish to be classed with the numerous swindlers of our city, and particularly desire every person to make inquiry about us before giving us an order. If this plan is always followed, honest men will be supported and swindlers die out.

This same 1895 catalog had more than 20 pages devoted to furniture, including upholstered parlor furniture; oak chamber suits (bedroom furniture), sideboards, kitchen cabinets, bookcases, desks, parlor stands, tables and chairs; lawn furniture, and rattan and reed furniture.

While Montgomery Ward and Company achieved continued success with their nationwide mail-order business, they were by no means the only house of this kind, and they received stiff competition from other compa-

nies—especially Sears, Roebuck and Company.

Sears, Roebuck and Company

Founded in 1886 by Richard Warren Sears, this young business was first known as R.W. Sears Watch Company. In 1887 Sears moved his mail-order watch business from Minneapolis to Chicago to take advantage of the large railroad network there. Once settled in his new location, Sears hired Alvah Curtis Roebuck (who later became a partner) as a watch repairman.

After experiencing several moves and corporate changes over the next few years, the company finally became known as Sears, Roebuck and Company in 1893. The first mail-order catalog issued under this new company name was approximately 200 pages in size. Over the next several years the catalog expanded, business grew, and Sears, Roebuck and Company became a familiar household name.

Along with furniture, the fall 1900 Sears, Roebuck and Company catalog also included drugs; veterinary supplies; watches and jewelry; photographic sup-

Hartman Furniture ad from the March 1914 *Woman's World* magazine.

$25 Worth of Goods for One Dollar Cash!

Great EASY-WAY-TO-PAY Catalog of 5,000 Wonderful Offers, Sent Free!

We are distributing immense quantities of Furniture, Carpets, Rugs, Sewing Machines, Go-Carts, Musical Instruments, Jewelry, Household Linens, etc., direct to the home on the famous People's "Easy-Way-to-Pay" plan. The products of the many factories and mills under our control are now being sold at sensational reductions.

Our enormous buying power enables us to offer you easiest terms, best values and many other special inducements not attainable anywhere else. The extent and variety of our stocks is absolutely amazing. Don't buy furniture or merchandise of any kind at any price, until you get our People's Easy-Way-to-Pay Catalog with all its wealth of wonderful bargains. The postage alone on this great big book costs us 12c—the book is yours free—for the asking.

Merchandise for the Millions!
We Trust You Privately

We ship millions of dollars' worth of goods to everybody, everywhere, on the easiest terms that anyone could possibly ask. We trust you privately—no notes, no security, no interest. In thousands of homes you hear them say, "It's easy to pay, the People's way." Your word is good here.

One or All of This $24.53 Lot
Shipped for $1

Please note the pictures and prices, the unbeatable values of the lot of goods shown here. This entire lot, marked down to $24.53, comprising Sewing Rocker, Library Table, 9x12-foot Brussels Rug, and Easy-Fold Go-Cart—crated and shipped direct to you on receipt of $1.00 cash; the balance you pay in little monthly amounts at your convenience. $50 worth of goods shipped for $2 cash.

The Book of Amazing Offers

Our People's Easy-Way-to-Pay Catalog enables you to secure all the furniture and household goods you want, for very little money. Every family ought to have this book. A postal brings it free, postpaid.

Embroidery Patterns FREE!

50 Embroidery Patterns FREE

We will send free with each People's Easy-to-Pay Book an assortment of fifty beautiful People's Embroidery Patterns while they last. These are the same quality of patterns that you pay at least 15c each for at any store.

Write Quick

before our supply of Free Patterns is exhausted. Get a copy of the People's Easy-Way-to-Pay Book and begin saving money at once. Take your choice of over 5,000 remarkable offers of everything used in the home. All on the People's Easy-Way-to-Pay Plan. Write for free catalog and 50 People's Embroidery Patterns today.

Library Table $6.65

$1.00 Cash Brings One or All

Sewing Rocker $2.98

9x12 ft. Brussels Rug $8.95

Folding Go-Cart $5.95

People's Outfitting Company
396 E Street, Detroit, Mich.

People's Outfitting Company ad from *Woman's World,* March 1914.

plies; talking machines; sporting goods and guns; bicycles; men's clothing, boots and shoes; toys and games; ladies clothing; hardware; stoves; harnesses and saddles; crockery and glassware; sewing machines; and baby carriages. The fall 1900 catalog would be mailed to any address upon receipt of 15 cents. Prices and merchandise were good for 12 months (the company was switching to an annual catalog distribution rather than semi-annual as they'd done previously). This change was instituted as a cost-saving measure and was explained in the front of the catalog, "in this way we hope to be able to reach every one of our customers with our latest catalogue, without putting them to the inconvenience and expense of sending twice a year for our book. At the same time we will save thousands of dollars that will go direct to our customers in the way of lower prices and better value."

The mail-order catalogs of the late nineteenth and early twentieth centuries were practically memorized, page after page, by rural American families who eagerly awaited their arrival and then poured over the latest fashions, home furnishings, housewares, tools, and other goods. This age of catalog fashion introduced a new era of country furnishings—sturdy, factory-made pieces that were stylish and yet dollar-wise and sensible for rural or small-town living.

While some of the changes in country furniture were born of ingenuity, modernization, machinery and mail-order shopping (wicker furniture and mail-order oak), other changes came about from the Victorian urbanite's desire to escape nineteenth-century industrialization. In their effort to once again be one with nature and look to the great outdoors for comfort and solitude, rustic twig furniture (also referred to as "Adirondack" furniture) outfitted resorts, mountain retreats and the great "camps" in which the Victorians sought refuge.

After looking at the diverse and ever-changing face of nineteenth- and early twentieth-century America, clearly there is more to the American country furniture category than just hand-crafted, painted or primitive pieces. It was middle-class Americans, heartland factories and rural dwellers that inspired and created the light and airy wicker produced well into the twentieth century, the twig furniture factory-produced in Indiana until the 1950s, and the massive oak (albeit in various styles) that furnished middle American parlors through the 1930s.

Front Porch Wicker

From the 1880s on, wicker furniture graced the front porches of homes all across America. Politics and crops were discussed, recipes were exchanged, and families would sit on the porch to visit with each other and with neighbors. The porch became a popular gathering place—an extension of the home—and wicker was the ideal furnishing since it was not only sturdy and comfortable, but weather resistant as well.

During the first half of the nineteenth century, wicker furnishings were imported from both England and the Far East for use inside the home. By 1855 the Wakefield Rattan Company of South Reading, Massachusetts, was

Wicker settee, painted white, 37″ wide × 36″ tall, **$125.**

Square-back wicker rocker, upholstered seat and back, flat arms, natural finish, 30″ wide × 24″ deep × 35″ tall, **$225.**

Child's wicker rocker with tapestry upholstered seat, 16″ wide × 14″ deep × 22″ tall, **$125.**

Wicker chair, upholstered cushion and back, Heywood-Wakefield tag, flat arms, 30″ wide × 26″ deep × 33″ tall, **$175.**

White wicker Lloyd loom chest with upholstered and padded top, made in England, 36″ wide × 20″ tall, **$155.**

113

Wicker rocker, natural finish, cushioned, 23″ wide × 38″ tall, **$125.**

Wicker chair painted green with a red floral cushion, part of a two-piece set (including a settee), 28″ wide × 28″ deep × 32″ tall, **$425 for the set.**

Wicker chair, part of a two-piece set (settee to match), upholstered green stripe cushion, 32″ wide × 28″ deep × 34″ tall, **$895 for the set.**

White six-leg wicker table with oval top, circa 1920s, 36″ wide × 26″ tall, **$125.**

A Heywood-Wakefield advertisement from the May 1925 *Delineator* magazine.

producing wicker, much of it ornate Victorian in style, full of curliques and decorative embellishments.

In the late 1880s the population in general was very concerned with cleanliness and sanitary surroundings, and wicker furnishings promoted good health with their open-weave design. Wicker furnishings were popular in the bedroom, parlor, and finally, on the front porch.

"Wicker" is a generic word used to describe furniture made of rattan, reed, willow, cane, or paper fiber. Initially,

115

YPSILANTI
Reed and FURNITURE
Fibre

So attractive are the new Ypsilanti patterns of reed and fibre furniture that to see is to desire to possess. From the great variety now available there are pieces suitable and serviceable for every room in your home.

The Ypsilanti line offers quality in finish and workmanship that cannot be excelled because Ypsilanti has unequaled advantages in plant facilities and experience.

Ypsilanti furniture is sold by more than 4,000 responsible dealers. The names of those nearest you will be sent on request.

YPSILANTI REED FURNITURE CO.
(Dept. B) Ionia, Mich.

Largest Makers of Reed and Fibre Furniture
Also Makers of Reed and Fibre Baby Carriages

A 1925 ad for Ypsilanti reed and fibre furniture.

when Cyrus Wakefield founded his company in 1855, the wicker furniture was made of cane fashioned around hardwood frames. He then went on to use reed in more decorative pieces. Most of this early wicker furniture was given a coat of varnish, but some pieces were painted in the then-popular colors of white, green, black and lavender.

As styles began to change, the wicker furnishings of the early 1900s took on a more simple appearance. The curliques of the Victorian era were replaced stylistically by an attractive al-

Wicker rocker with Art Deco diamond design on back, cushioned, painted yellow, 28″ wide × 28″ deep × 30″ tall, **$75.**

though less ornate latticework design (which also served as a cost-cutting measure since production was less involved). This wicker design became extremely popular at hotels and resorts, and it wasn't long before manufacturers labeled styles accordingly. For example, some wicker pieces were known as "Bar Harbor," "Newport," "Southampton," and "Cape Cod." The Bar Harbor style is recognized by thick reeds, square backs, flat arms and an open-weave criss-cross design. Newport and Southampton refer to chairs with heart-shaped or curved backs. Cape Cod wicker was constructed of tightly woven reed. Collectors should note that all of the open-weave porch or resort wicker of this era (as mentioned previously) is often collectively referred to as Bar Harbor wicker.

Mission-style wicker furnishings with close-weave construction and ample square shape also was produced during the early 1900s (1900–1920). Many of these pieces had upholstered cushions, and the entire style was one of natural simplicity.

The manufacture of wicker fur-nishings changed drastically in 1917 with the invention of the Lloyd loom. Marshall Lloyd, who manufactured baby carriages, created the new loom, which wove machine-made strands of paper or paper-fiber, into sheets which could be wrapped around furniture. Lloyd's search for a way to continue production of baby carriages in the midst of a shortage of supplies ultimately revolutionized the wicker furniture industry. In just three short years after the invention of this loom, half of all wicker furniture in the United States was being turned out by the Lloyd loom process. The Lloyd Manufacturing Company continued operations until 1921, at which time the company became a part of the Heywood-Wakefield Company. These machine-made furnishings were produced mainly for indoor use, and many of the circa 1920–1930 pieces were outfitted with colorful chintz cushions. They were quite popular in the parlor and screened porches or sun rooms, and the square or boxy lines became quite fashionable. The manufactured wicker furniture was, however, not as comfortable as hand-

117

made pieces (the machine-made furniture did not have the elasticity or "give" of the natural materials) and inferior woods were often used in construction.

Art Deco invaded wicker furniture when manufacturers began incorporating a geometric diamond-like design in the backs of chairs and settees, on table aprons and elsewhere during the 1920s and 1930s.

Wicker was still being painted dur-

Wicker settee, chair, rocker and table (set also includes a plant stand), circa 1930s, original finish, **$975 for the set.**

Settee from set pictured previously, 45″ wide × 32″ tall.

White wicker porch rocker with open-weave back, 21" wide × 43" tall, **$140.**

White wicker porch rocker with replaced seat, 22" wide × 50" tall, **$175.**

White wicker planter, 24" long × 24" tall, **$95.**

ing the early 1900s, and along with the popular white and green, pieces were also painted in blues and reds.

By the mid-1930s the sale of wicker furnishings was on the decline. While the Lloyd loom process had brought increased productivity and cost-cutting measures to wicker furniture manufacture (thus lowering furni-

ture prices), the quality found in the early handcrafted (from natural materials) pieces was lacking. In addition, the public was growing tired of this furniture type as new, modernistic styles captured their attention.

From the time wicker was first made in the United States in the 1850s until the end of its popularity by the

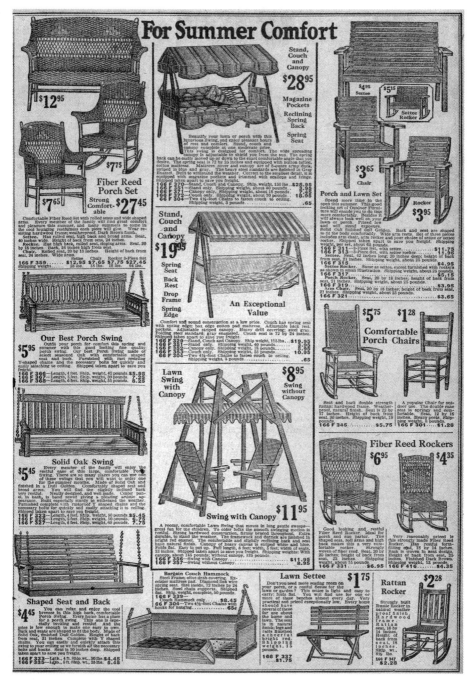

This page from a 1924 Montgomery Ward catalog offered a variety of porch swings, chairs and rockers.

Wicker chair, "hard to come by" shape with upholstered seat and back, 30" wide × 28" deep × 38" tall, **$275.**

1930s (note that there were wicker "revivals" during the mid-twentieth century and again during the 1980s), well over 100 different companies worldwide manufactured and/or sold wicker in America. Imported wicker arrived from England, France, Germany, Austria, Holland, Switzerland and Belgium.

Along with the Wakefield Rattan Company of South Reading, Massachusetts, which became Heywood Brothers and Wakefield Company after an 1897 merger (and was the world's biggest producer of wicker furniture), some other American companies producing wicker furniture included: The Boston Willow Furniture Company of Boston, Massachusetts; Joseph P. McHugh, Bielecky Brothers, Messrs. J. and C. Berrian, and Grand Central Wicker Shop, Inc., all of New York City; Ficks Reed Company of Cincinnati, Ohio; Northfield Company of Sheboygan, Wisconsin; Ypsilanti Reed Furniture Company, Ionia, Michigan; S. Karpen and Brothers, Charles W.H. Frederick,

Western Rattan Company, and George J. Schmidt and Brother, all of Chicago, Illinois; Chittenden and Eastman Company of Burlington, Iowa; and Memphis Furniture Manufacturing Company of Memphis, Tennessee.

Wicker furnishings were available through furniture stores and mail-order catalogs. For example, the Montgomery Ward and Company spring/summer 1895 catalog included a section on lawn furniture and one on rattan and reed furniture.

One lawn furniture selection described a "Ladies Veranda Rocker," "back and seat is made of reed, posts are made of hardwood, is nicely varnished; well made and cheap. Weight, about 14 pounds. Price only $1.85."

The rattan and reed furniture pages included a large selection of rockers and chairs for the parlor, many of them quite fancy with decorative Victorian fan-backs, heart-backs and curliques.

In a replica of the 1898–1899 Heywood Brothers and Wakefield Company catalog (from Dover Publications Inc., New York, 1982), wicker authority Richard Saunders notes in the Introduction that "by the time the firm of Heywood Brothers and Wakefield Company was incorporated, the public had fully accepted wicker furniture on all fronts—the porch, the garden, the sitting room and the bedroom. Not only had wicker's three-dimensional, airy quality won the public over, but its sheer adaptability seemed to suit the age."

This catalog offered the public a variety of their favorite wicker pieces, including the fancy and ornate, the simple and airy design of the open criss-cross weave, and also a fine selection of Morris chairs with upholstered cushions.

The 1924 Montgomery Ward and

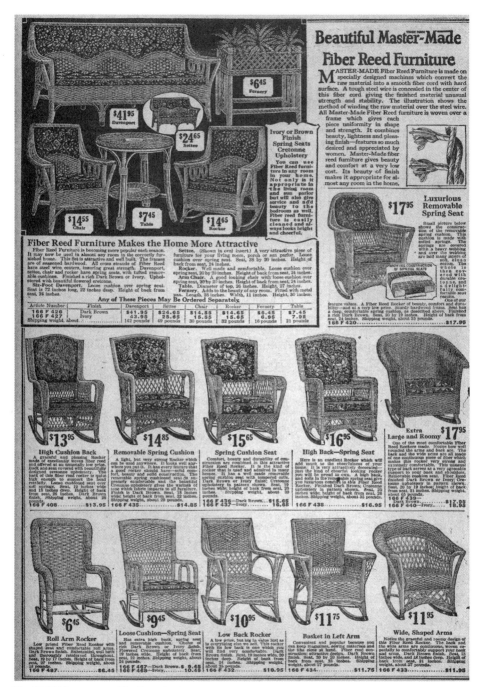

The 1924 Montgomery Ward catalog included an extensive selection of machine-made "Master-Made Reed Furniture."

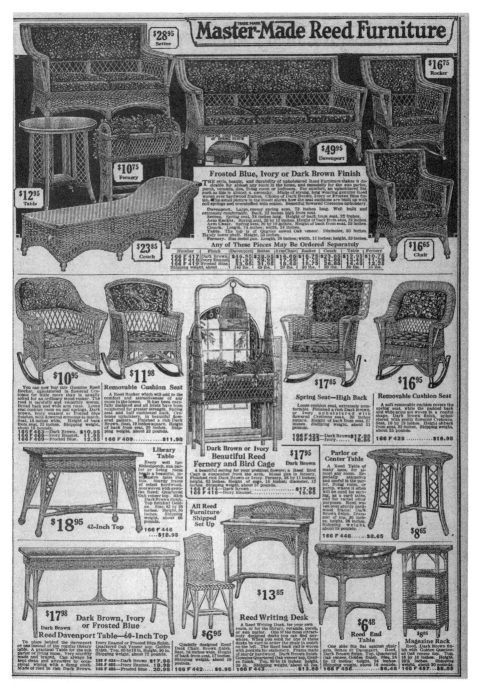

A second page of "Master-Made Reed Furniture" available through Montgomery Ward mail-order.

Hints on Wicker Furniture

Inspect old wicker carefully to be sure it is structurally sound. Older pieces are heavier since they were constructed with a hardwood (usually oak or maple) frame.

In order to recognize the material used in wicker furnishings (which can often help date a piece), remember that reed, which was used quite often prior to 1900, is straight with a round shape and often-visible grain; cane is also straight, but flat; and machine-made paper fiber looks just like thick string and is often wrapped around wire (typically not visible) to lend it support.

Old wicker furnishings finished with a coat of varnish are the most desirable pieces but are becoming hard to find. Much old wicker was painted, and has often been repainted, but beware of reproductions which are lightweight compared to the real thing and often constructed with staples rather than nails. Old wicker will show signs of age, so inspect for worn feet and missing or loose bits of wicker. Vintage wicker chairs, tables, plant stands and children's chairs/rockers are easy to find while other pieces are scarce.

Repairing wicker can be costly. If you buy a piece with a tear in the seat or worn/damaged spots, find someone experienced to fix it. A reputable dealer who knows wicker should be able to recommend someone.

Wicker chair with original tapestry fabric, 24″ wide × 28″ deep × 30″ tall, **$245.**

Company catalog offered a variety of wicker furnishings, including their "Beautiful Master-Made Fiber Reed Furniture." The catalog explained this furniture was

> *Made on specially designed machines which convert the raw material into a smooth fiber cord with hard surface. A tough steel wire is concealed in the center of this fiber cord giving the finished material unusual strength and stability. All Master-Made Fiber Reed furniture is woven over a frame which gives each piece uniformity in shape and strength. It combines beauty, lightness and pleasing finish—features so much desired and appreciated by women.*

This same 1924 catalog offered a three-piece fiber reed porch set (settee, chair and rocker) for $27.45. The set had a wear-resistant hardwood frame, was weatherproof, and had a dark-brown finish. Other pieces available for indoor use were offered with a frosted blue, ivory or dark-brown finish. Cushioned seats and backs on chairs and rockers were offered in abundance, and a quarter-sawed oak veneer top was standard on the library table, 60″ davenport table, desk and end table advertised.

Oak Furniture

From the late 1800s through the 1920s, factory-made oak furniture was popular with the growing middle class. These sturdy furnishings were affordable and readily available all across the country, thanks to mail-order catalogs, which revolutionized the way shopping needs could be met.

Golden oak rocker, pressed-back design of flowers and heart, original seat, 21″ wide × 19″ deep × 40″ tall, **$138.**

The wide selection and diversity of pieces available meant that an entire country home could be furnished in oak if so desired. Oak cupboards, iceboxes and tables were made for the kitchen; three-piece sets, tables, chairs and rockers were made for the parlor; chamber suits could outfit the bedroom; and desks, bookcases and hall trees could fill the needs of the rest of the house.

While factory-made oak (and oak look-alike) furnishings were manufactured all across the country, several noted manufacturers were located in Grand Rapids, Michigan. As a result, these furnishings are sometimes generically referred to as "Grand Rapids" furnishings. The Industrial Revolution of the late 1800s ushered in machinery that could quickly and precisely saw wood, create joints and stamp or steampress decorations such as those found on pressed-back chairs.

Most oak furniture was produced from trees categorized as either red oak (which is pale pink-brown in appearance) or white oak (which is a light tan). The wood was either quartersawed or plain-sawed. Quarter-sawed oak has a curved wood grain and is stronger than plain-sawed oak since it shrinks and warps less. A quarter-sawed log was first divided into four sections and then boards were cut, whereas

Painted oak pressed-back highchair (pictured without tray), 13″ wide × 36″ tall, **$40.**

Golden oak lamp table with splayed legs, 20″ wide × 20″ deep × 29″ tall, **$150.**

Golden oak lamp table, 24″ wide × 24″ deep × 28″ tall, **$98.**

plain-sawed boards were cut lengthwise from the whole log. Plain-sawed oak exhibits stripes or a straight-grain pattern.

Oak look-alikes were also used quite often in furniture production, and it sometimes can be difficult to distinguish oak from one of its imitiators. The most common oak look-alikes include ash, elm and chestnut. While all three were used in furniture construction, ash is often found in wooden iceboxes, elm was often used in producing veneer, and chestnut was an oak substitute in a wide assortment of pieces. Chestnut is recognizable by its grayish-brown appearance and lack of a typical oak grain.

Oak furnishings were given either a "golden oak" clear varnish finish, which was very popular during the

Golden oak table with brass ball and claw feet, 22″ wide × 22″ deep × 30″ tall, **$225.**

Golden oak fern stand, 20″ wide × 30″ tall, **$160.**

Round quarter-sawn oak table, claw feet, two leaves, 60″, **$600 ($995 for table and four oak chairs).**

Square oak table with three leaves, 72″ long, **$500;** six T-back chairs with leather seats, **$300;** crock on the table, **$350.**

Golden oak side-by-side, 40″ wide × 12″ deep × 66″ tall, **$895.**

Golden oak sideboard with mirror and fancy trim, 44″ wide × 20″ deep × 74″ tall, **$625.**

Oak three-drawer dresser, 34" wide × 30" tall, **$250.**

Oak chest of drawers with carved walnut pulls, 40" wide × 17" deep × 43" tall, **$450.**

Oak chest of drawers with bowed front, 30" wide × 42" tall, **$375.**

1890s and early 1900s, or an "antique" finish, which was achieved through the use of a dark stain.

While numerous different companies produced oak furniture well into the 1930s, a small sampling includes the following manufacturers: Berkey and Gay, Century Furniture Company, Grand Rapids Bookcase and Chair Company, Grand Rapids Chair Company, Grand Rapids Furniture Company, Johnson-Handley-Johnson, Luce Furniture Company, Phoenix Furniture Company, Royal Furniture Company, Johnson Furniture Company, Imperial Table Company, Kindel Bed Company and the Macey Company (all of Grand Rapids, Michigan); Baker Furniture Factories of Allegan, Michigan; Basic Furniture Company of Waynesboro, Virginia; Empire Furniture of Rockford, Illinois; Kensington Manufactur-

Text continued on page 137

A Larkin Company ad from the March 1914 *Woman's World* magazine.

This New-Style Credit

Is Used to Furnish 1,666 Homes a Day

Your Credit Card Will Come With Your Catalog

No References Required

We now give credit to home lovers without any red tape. No references, no contract, no security. Ask for our catalog and your credit card will go with it. You will then have an open charge account and can order what you wish.

We furnish an average of 1,666 homes per day for people on these easy terms.

Pay 3 Cents a Day

Goods are all sent on 30 days' approval. You have a month to return anything not wanted, and we'll pay freight both ways.

Take a year to pay for the goods you keep. Pay as convenient—a little each month. If sickness comes or loss of work we will gladly extend the time.

You can furnish a home in beautiful shape by saving 2 or 3 cents a day.

What You Save

We sell at cash prices on credit, and no interest is charged. We guarantee to save you from 15 to 50 per cent under any cash prices in catalogs or stores. If we don't do that, return the goods.

We do this by enormous buying, and by selling direct to an average of 1,666 homes a day. We take whole factory outputs, buy up surplus stocks. We sell hundreds of things at just one-half store prices.

Five Costly Books Free

Our Spring Furniture Book pictures 5,112 things for the home. Many are pictured in actual colors. This mammoth book costs us $1 per copy, but we send it free.

We issue four other big catalogs, named in the coupon. Ask for any you want. See our styles, our variety, our prices. You will be amazed.

Mail this coupon for the books you want and your credit card will go with them. Do this today. Cut out the coupon now.

Fabricord Leather Rocker $5.45

50c With Order
50c Monthly

Notice the handsome heart-shaped back with ruffled edges, and the roomy seat is 19 inches deep and 21 inches wide. Fabricord leather covering is guaranteed. Entire frame is well made of selected hard wood. Weight about 75 lbs.

This is a Great Bargain

No. 50D4B151. Price, $5.45

Spiegel, May, Stern Co

1336 W. 35th Street, Chicago

5,112 Things TO CHOOSE FROM

Furniture
Carpets—Rugs
Oilcloths, etc.
Draperies
Baby Cabs
Blankets—Linens

Silverware
Chinaware
Sewing Machines
Bicycles—Toys
Cameras—Guns
Pictures—Clocks

A YEAR TO PAY

Get Martha Lane Adams' Book of Spring Styles for Women

SPIEGEL, MAY, STERN CO. (678)
1336 W. 35th Street, Chicago
Mail me free your **Spring Furniture Book.**
Also send me books marked below.
[ ] Stove Book.   [ ] Dress Goods.
[ ] Watches and Jewelry.
[ ] Spring Styles for Women.

Name _____

Address _____
Write plainly. Give full address.
Check which catalogs you want.

The March 1914 *Woman's World* magazine also included this ad for Spiegel, May, Stern Company, which boasted a catalog of furniture with over 5,112 items for the home.

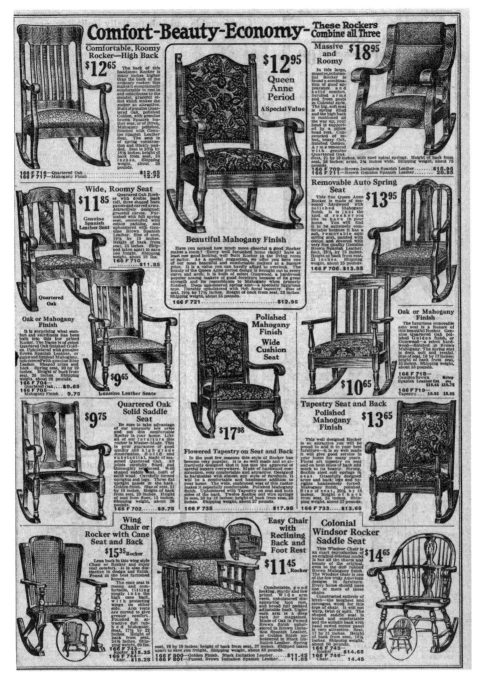

A fine selection of oak rockers from a 1924 Montgomery Ward catalog.

Distinctive Queen Anne Rocker $10.63

Quartered Oak Golden Finish or Hardwood Brown Mahogany Finish

This Rocker has all the qualities that you look for in good furniture. Beauty of design and finish, soundness of construction, and luxurious ease and comfort. Yet it is moderate in price. Designed in the graceful and ever popular Queen Anne style. Removable auto seat, over nine coil springs, is covered with Blue Genuine Leather or Figured Tapestry. This rocker will give you lasting service. Height of back from seat, 22 inches. Seat, 17 by 19¼ inches. This rocker may be had in either quartered Oak, finished a rich Golden, or in select Hardwood, finished Brown Mahogany. State finish wanted. Shipping weight, about 36 pounds.

Tapestry or Genuine Leather Seat

	Oak	Mahogany
166 F 738—Blue Genuine Leather	$10.60	$10.65
166 F 740—Figured Tapestry	10.63	10.63

Sewing Rocker
An Ideal Gift for Mother
$5.85

This Rocker with padded seat and restful back will give greatest comfort while sewing. Conveniently placed under the seat is a large sewing compartment with safety catch.

Of seasoned Solid Oak in Fumed Brown or Golden finish. Size of seat, 17 by 16 inches. Height of back from seat, 22 inches. Front posts, 1¼ inches square. Shipped set up. Shipping weight, about 16 pounds.

166 F 562—Golden..............$5.85
166 F 563—Fumed Brown..... 5.95

Comfortable and Substantially Built Rockers

Quartered Oak — **Form Fitting Seat** — **Bent Arm Rocker**

$6.48

An all around strong, serviceable Rocker. Notice the well shaped construction of the comfortable seat. Built of Oak with Quartered Oak veneer seat and back. Finished a Golden Gloss. It is made with form fitting back and arms which add greatly to its comfort giving qualities. Seat, 19½ by 19¾ inches; height of back from seat, 24 inches. Shipped taken apart. Shipping weight, about 25 pounds.
166 F 911..............$6.48

Solid Oak Rocker
$4.48

This Rocker is an exceptional value. Made of Solid Oak, Golden finish, with veneered form fitting seat and comfortable arms. Has six well matched panels in back. It is strongly made and braced throughout, giving you long service at a low price. Seat, 19½ by 19 inches. Height of back from seat, 24 inches. Shipped taken apart to save you freight. Shipping weight, about 20 pounds.
166 F 912..............$4.48

$4.75

Comfort, sound construction and low price mean big value in this Rocker. It is very carefully made of seasoned hardwood, finished imitation Golden Quartered Oak. Shaped seat and broad well shaped back and arm rests. Seat, 21 by 18 inches. Height of back from seat, 26 inches. Shipped set up. Shipping weight, about 20 pounds.
166 F 915..............$4.75

Ideal Rocker for the Sewing Room or Spare Bedroom — **Solid Oak**

$3.55

This very sturdy and serviceable Rocker is made of Solid Oak, strongly built and finished Golden or Fumed Brown. Wood shaped seat; 5 flat spindles in back. Size of seat, 16½ by 15 inches; height of back from seat, 19½ inches. Shipped set up. Shipping weight, about 14 pounds.
166 F 924—Golden..........$3.55
166 F 925—Fumed Brown.. 3.65

An Extra Rocker is a Necessary Part of Every Household — **Imitation Quartered Oak**

$2.98

Seasoned hardwood, finished imitation Quartered Golden Oak. A fine sewing or bedroom Rocker that will come in handy anywhere. Size of seat, 16 by 14 inches; height of back from seat, 21 inches. Shipped set up. Shipping weight, about 15 pounds.
166 F 926..............$2.98

Low Priced Rocker

$2.78

Sewing Rocker with 5 flat spindles in back, neatly turned posts and stretcher and shaped seat. A very good rocker at this price, strongly made of select hardwood. Golden finish. Seat, 16 by 16 inches; height of back from seat, 21 inches. Shipped set up. Shipping weight, about 12 pounds.
166 F 923..............$2.78

$11.85

High Back Head Rest

Built of Oak in Golden or Fumed Brown finish. Spring seat. High back is heavily cushioned and has pillow style head rest. Upholstered in Brown Imitation Spanish Leather. Size of seat, 21 by 20 inches; height of back from seat, 25 inches. Front posts, 1¾ inches square. Shipped taken apart. Shipping weight, about 55 pounds.
166 F 577—Fumed Brown..$11.85
166 F 579—Golden.......... 11.95

$13.75

Genuine Spanish Leather

Large, massive, Oak Rocker in mission design. Fumed Brown finish. Spring seat is built up over oil tempered coil springs. Thickly cushioned back. Brown Genuine Spanish Leather upholstery. Seat, 20 by 19 inches; height of back from seat, 25 inches. The arms are 4½ inches wide. Shipped taken apart. Shipping weight, about 65 pounds.
166 F 595..............$13.75

$7.95

Wing Back Design

A Mission Rocker of seasoned Oak, finished a pleasing Fumed Brown. Back shows a rather unusual design with scrolled side wings. Spring seat is deeply cushioned and the back well padded. Brown Imitation Spanish Leather. Below the cushion back are 6 flat banisters, adding strength and beauty. The spring seat is 19½ by 18½ inches; height of back from seat is 23 inches. Shipped taken apart to save you freight. Shipping weight, about 50 pounds.
166 F 572..............$7.95

Cushioned Back and Seat—Good Value

$8.95

A Rocker we are glad to recommend for comfort and durability. The scroll design of this rocker is artistically carried out in the Oak wings, arms and posts which are finished in Golden. The cushioning of both seat and back is designed to give a great degree of comfort, yet retain its firmness and round shape. Durable Brown Imitation Spanish Leather upholstery; cushioned spring seat and divided back; all surfaces plain and easy to keep clean. Seat, 19 by 20 inches; height of back from seat, 25 inches. Shipped taken apart to save you freight. Shipping weight, about 40 pounds.
166 F 812..............$8.95

Reclining Upholstered Rocker
$11.85

Golden Finish

Foot Rest for Comfort

Brown Imitation Spanish Leather

Adjustable Reclining Back

Enjoy real comfort in one of these reclining upholstered Rockers. Everything about this chair makes you want to sit down and rest. The well padded cushion seat, the upholstered reclining back, the disappearing foot rest and the broad arm supports all invite you to perfect relaxation. By moving a convenient support up or down, you may raise or lower the back to the position that is most comfortable. By pulling out the foot rest you may stretch out at ease. Strongly built of Seasoned Oak in Golden finish. Quartered oak wings. Well padded spring seat, 19½ by 19 inches; adjustable wing back, 29 inches from seat. Arm rests, 4½ inches wide. Upholstered in Brown Imitation Spanish Leather. Shipped taken apart to save you freight. Shipping weight, about 75 pounds.
166 F 300..............$11.85

$7.48

High Back Oak Rocker

Notice how sturdily this Genuine Oak Mission Rocker is built. It is thoroughly reinforced and so well made that it will last you for many years. Comfortable spring seat built over oil tempered spirals and thickly padded. Covered with Brown Imitation Spanish Leather. Broad comfortable arms. Fumed Brown finish. Size of seat, 19½ by 19 inches; height of back from seat, 33 inches. Front posts are 1¾ inches square. Shipped taken apart to save you freight. Shipping weight, about 55 pounds.
166 F 534..............$7.48

$7.95

Wing Back Rocker

A luxurious Rocker with spring cushioned seat and cushioned back. The back with its well designed wings will add greatly to your personal comfort. Tempered coil springs in the seat. Built of seasoned Oak with shicks of finish and upholstery. Size of seat, 18 by 18 inches; height of back from seat, 23 inches. Shipped taken apart to save you freight. Shipping weight, about 50 pounds. Brown Imitation Spanish Leather back. Seat is 19 by 19 inches.
166 F 700—Golden Finish; Black Imitation Leather..............$7.95
166 F 701—Fumed Finish; Brown Imitation Spanish Leather..$8.45

$4.65

Scrolled Back Rocker

Comfort, soundness of construction and durability make this Rocker a big value at the low price we ask for it. A very pleasing scrolled effect in center panel of the back. Rocker is of Solid Oak, Fumed Brown finish, and well built of seasoned stock. The seat is well cushioned and comfortable. The broad arm rests add to its value. Shipping weight, about 40 pounds.
166 F 516..............$4.65

More oak rockers from a 1924 Montgomery Ward catalog.

133

Genuine Oak Living Room Set

$2⁹⁸

$2⁹⁷

$3³³

↑ Arm Rocker

566M512—
Sale price.............$2.98
Size of seat, 19x19 in.
Height of back from seat, 20 in. Ship. wt., about 27 lbs.
Genuine Oak, in Fumed Brown finish, Artificial Spanish Leather seat.

The Table

566M514—
Sale price.............$3.33
Size of top, 34x23 in. Ship. wt., about 45 lbs.
Built of Genuine Oak in Fumed brown finish. Note the handy book racks on each end and the shelf on bottom. Books shown are not included.

Arm Chair ↑

566M516—
Sale price $2.97
Size of seat, 19x19 in. Height of back from seat, 20 in. Ship. wt., about 27 lbs.
Genuine Oak in Fumed brown finish. Durable artificial Spanish Leather seat. Full size and comfortable.

566M518—
Sale price $1.98
Size of seat, 17x15 in. Height of back from seat, 20½ in. Ship. wt., about 17 lbs.
Genuine Oak in Fumed brown finish. Artificial Spanish Leather seat. Ideal for sewing rocker.

$1⁹⁸

Get the Complete Set

When you stop to consider, you will wonder how so good a suite as this can be solidly built of Genuine Oak and nicely finished and sold for so little money. It will give you a lot of service.

All 5 Pieces
Sale Price
$12⁹⁸
566M522

We have sold many thousands of these Genuine Oak suites in previous sales and they have given universal satisfaction. This big volume of business enables us to make special contracts for their production that we save you considerable money on the price.

566M520—
Sale price $1.97
Size of seat, 17x15 in. Height of back from seat, 20½ in. Ship. wt., about 17 lbs.
Genuine Oak in Fumed finish. Artificial Spanish Leather seat. Block braced and glued. Very strong.

$1⁹⁷

A Restful $6⁴⁸ Rocker

566M530—
Sale price...............$6.48
Size of seat, 19x18 in. Height of back from seat, 26 in. Ship. wt., about 70 lbs.
Comfort Rocker, with reclining roomy back, foot rest and yielding spring seat. You will enjoy it, for you can lean back with the back reclined to the angle which best suits you, and really rest. Built of Genuine Oak in the popular Golden finish. Upholstered in dependable Artificial Spanish Leather. Fastened by springs to floor base. Rocks with an easy swinging motion.

$3⁹⁸ **Genuine Oak** Golden Finish

566M532—Sale price..$3.98
Size of seat, 19½x18 in. Height of back from seat, 24 in. Ship. wt., about 45 lbs.
Built of Genuine Oak in the pleasing Golden finish. Upholstered with durable Artificial Spanish Leather. Has spring seat. Built solid and strong, with broad arms, and so proportioned as to be very restful. You will like the rocker itself as well as the low sale price.

All goods on this page shipped from stock at Chicago

$2¹⁸ ←

566M540—
Sale price...$2.18
Size of seat, 19x18 in. Height of back from seat, 24 in. Ship. wt., about 29 lbs.
Built of seasoned hardwood, in imitation Quartered Golden Oak finish. Saddle shaped seat. Comfortable back, with broad panels. Very strongly braced base. Shaped arms. Fancy turned spindles and posts. The quality will please and the sale price saves you money.

69c
566M542
Top, 13¾x10¾ in. Ship. wt., about 6 lbs. Can be sent by parcel post.
Genuine Oak, Fumed finish. Artificial Spanish Leather top. Strong and durable.

$8⁸⁵ →

566M544
Artificial Spanish Leather ..$8.85
566M546
Genuine Spanish Leather ..$9.98
Size of seat, 21x20 in. Height of back from seat, 26 in. Ship. wt., about 60 lbs.
Very massive Genuine Oak comfort rocker, in rich Golden finish. Highly polished. Yielding spring seat. A rocker you will appreciate in your own home.

A page from the 1918 Montgomery Ward catalog offering a fine selection of oak furnishings.

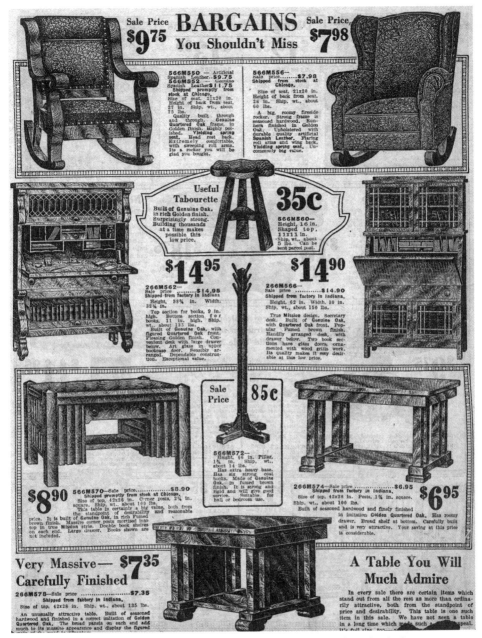

Also from the 1918 Montgomery Ward catalog, this page depicts a variety of oak pieces.

Oak chest of drawers, 33″ wide × 18″ deep × 40″ tall, **$189.**

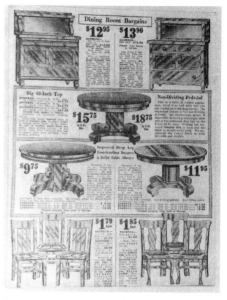

These 1918 oak dining room furnishings could be bought through the Montgomery Ward catalog.

Oak commode with towel bar, 32″ wide × 18″ deep × 50″ tall, **$265.**

Small Eastlake-style oak table with incised lines, 17″ wide × 32″ tall, **$125.**

Oak bookshelf with pressed-back leaf design, folds up for storage, 24″ wide × 9″ deep × 44″ tall, **$150.**

ing Company of New York, New York; Henry C. Steul and Sons and Kittinger Furniture Company of Buffalo, New York; Batesville Cabinet Company of Batesville, Indiana; William A. French Furniture Company of Minneapolis, Minnesota; Charles P. Limbert Company and Ottawa Furniture Company of Holland, Michigan; J.D. Bassett Manufacturing Company, Bassett, Virginia; Saginaw Furniture Shops, Saginaw, Michigan; Steinman and Meyer Furniture Company of Cincinnati, Ohio; J.L. Strassel Company of Louisville, Kentucky; The Hoosier Manufacturing Company, New Castle, Indiana; and Come-Pact Furniture Company of Toledo, Ohio. Many small furniture shops located in New York State and Michigan also turned out a great deal of Mission-style oak furnishings.

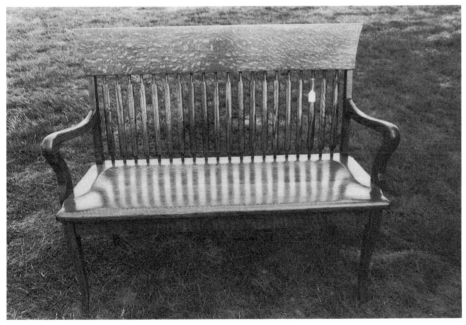

Golden oak bench, 44″ long × 18″ wide × 38″ tall, **$475.**

Mail-order sales of oak furniture skyrocketed between 1900 and the late 1920s. The Montgomery Ward and Company 1895 catalog No. 57 included more than 20 pages offering oak furnishings, and by 1908 the Sears Roebuck catalog included 60 pages depicting oak or other hardwood pieces.

Along with the furniture stores and the booming mail-order business, oak furnishings and accessories also could be obtained as product premiums. For example, the Larkin Company of Buffalo, New York, advertised in the March 1914 edition of *Woman's World* magazine

> *Your home made cozy without extra cost . . . think, Mrs. Lover of a cozy home, how fine a rocker would look in that living room of yours! Wouldn't you phone your druggist to send it to you quick if you thought he'd give it to you without extra charge as a saving with your regular purchases? By the Larkin Plan you can get this rocker or your choice of a thousand other handsome furnishings without extra charge . . . these articles are what you gain by buying your needed household supplies (foods, toilet preparations, soaps and notions) direct from us, the manufacturers and saving the expense and profits of the middlemen.*

The advertisement went on to explain that the three most popular ways to get Larkin premiums were to join a Larkin club and take turns with other members in receiving premiums, organize a Larkin club among friends and neighbors and earn premiums by sending in orders, or order supplies just for yourself and your family and get premiums with every purchase.

The Larkin Company spring 1914

Golden oak drop-front desk, 30″ wide × 12″ deep × 60″ tall, **$375.**

catalog included over 700 household supplies and more than 2000 premium articles, such as furniture, rugs, and clothing, which could be earned by buying them.

A sampling of oak furniture prices from various catalogs published between the late 1890s and mid-1920s are testimony to the fact that oak furnishings were indeed a good bargain. For example, in the Montgomery Ward and Company 1897 catalog, a three-piece oak chamber suit (double bed headboard and footboards, dresser with French legs and 24-inch by 30-inch bevel mirror, and washstand with towel bar) cost $21.80; a quarter-sawed oak hall tree with hand-carved embellishments and a 12-inch by 12-inch French bevel mirror cost $10.90; a quarter-

Hints on Oak Furniture

Oak furniture was the favorite of middle-class Americans for many years because it was affordable, sturdy and stylish. As a result, much of it is available today. Examine pieces carefully to determine sound construction and that the finish, hardware, and mirrors are in good condition. Inspect the inside of a case piece to make sure that it, too, is in good shape. Ask questions of the dealer and look at the piece carefully to determine if it is oak, an oak look-alike, or hardwood with an oak finish.

Some manufacturers attached labels to their goods or signed/inscribed them, so check for markings. Be aware that while vintage oak is readily available, some pieces are scarce or more difficult to come by (such as roll-top desks) and reproductions often fill the void.

Oak furniture is priced according to rarity, condition, design or style; and whether or not the piece incorporates features such as art glass, beveled mirrors, and carved, applied or pressed-back designs. Recently, Mission oak has been especially popular, keeping in mind the law of supply and demand, prices for this particular style of oak furnishings have been on the increase.

sawed oak table (top 18 by 33 inches) cost $3.75; and a side-by-side (combination bookcase and desk) with oak finish and French bevel mirror cost $9.95.

The Sears, Roebuck and Company catalog of fall 1900 offered pressed-back rock elm dining chairs for 68 cents apiece, while a solid oak example was priced $1.49. This same catalog offered an ornate pressed-back oak rocker with a leather seat for $3.00; a six-foot oak pillar extension table was $6.25; and an oak sideboard with mirror priced at $12.75.

In 1918 Montgomery Ward and Company offered bargains such as a massive library table (made of seasoned hardwood with a golden quarter-sawed oak finish) specially priced at $7.35 and a round six-foot oak table with an octagonal pedestal for $9.75.

In the 1924 Montgomery Ward and Company catalog, an oak Queen Anne rocker with tapestry or leather seat cost $10.63; a high-back oak Mission rocker was priced $7.48; an oak wardrobe cost $27.95; and a hardwood kitchen cupboard (oak finish) with glass doors was $14.95.

Rustic Twig Furniture

Rustic twig furnishings were made in America as early as the 1820s but did not reach the peak of their popularity until many years later.

With the growing Industrial Revolution came rapid urbanization. Factories appeared almost overnight; of the 1,750,000 immigrants that entered the country between 1840–1850, many ended up working 12 to 14 hours a day in textile mills and on assorted assembly/production lines. Many immigrants lived in poverty, and the growing cities were suddenly becoming a place to escape from, if even only for a little while. As a result, from the late 1870s through the 1930s, there was a "back to nature" movement in which city, state and national parks were established and resorts and private "camps" became the rage, especially in the Adirondack Mountains of New York State. These camps were usually owned by wealthy families and served as summer havens from city life. A camp was large enough to accommodate several guests and usually had a main lodge with a full-length front porch. The rustic twig furnishings in the camps were often crafted by artisans and those who lived year-round in the mountains, such as trappers, guides, and others.

Rustic twig furniture was also

Rustic planter of twig construction, 14″ wide × 33″ tall, **$70.**

made by the Amish, by gypsies that traveled the Midwest and southern states, and was factory-produced by several different midwestern companies.

Rustic furniture was crafted from an assortment of woods, including hickory, spruce, ash, elm, birch, laurel, apple, cedar and willow. Most pieces, made with branches, burls, knots and forks, were left natural, but the occasional decoration was added to Adirondack furnishings by using white bark or a design created from small twigs.

American-made rustic furnishings are categorized according to style/design, woods used in construction, and/or predominant provenance. They were popular for many years because they first served to remind late nineteenth-

Adirondack highchair, 14″ wide × 13″ deep × 40″ tall, **$185.**

Garden bench with traces of old blue paint, 42″ wide × 20″ deep × 32″ tall, **$145.**

Unusual pillow-back rustic rocker with rockers bolted to chair legs, 22″ wide × 48″ tall, **$175.**

Doll's twig rocker, 10″ wide × 15″ tall, **$38.**

mosaic twig work. White birch tree bark was also used to enhance these furnishings, which were created by both skilled and unskilled craftsmen. Along with the mountain region of New York State, Adirondack furniture also filled the resorts in New England and the Great Lakes area, but the Adirondack Mountains was the center of production for this particular style of casual furnishing.

Gypsy Rustic Furnishings

These were often made of willow, with chairs characterized by straight arms and legs made of peeled branches (often called pole chairs) with a loop-back.

Appalachian Twig Furniture

Named after the mountain region where they originated, Appalachian furnishings were crafted from willow, hickory and laurel. Between the late 1800s

century Victorians of nature in all her glory, and they also symbolized the "natural" aspect of the early 1900s Arts and Crafts movement. They were simplistic, comfortable and virtually maintenance-free. As a result we consider rustic furnishings in the following categories:

Early Rustic/Gothic Style

These twig furnishings were first used in English gardens. Benches, chairs and planters made of roots and branches could be seen in the United States by 1840. For example, the Niagara Falls Rustique Manufacturing Company, an early manufacturer founded in the 1840s, crafted twig tete-a-tetes, chairs, settees, benches and more than 70 different types of rustic planters.

Adirondack Furniture

The most noted of all rustic twig furnishings, Adirondack pieces often incorporated geometric designs using

Rustic hickory armchair, 20″ wide × 32″ tall, **135.**

Twig rocker with fabric seat, 22″ wide × 18″ deep × 32″ tall, **$235.**

son chair for $2.75 and included a selection of settees, stools, tables, couches, swings, beds, dressers, chiffoniers, stands, buffets, hatracks, and children's furnishings.

During the early 1900s the Old Hickory Chair Company shipped their goods all over the country—to department stores and especially to mountain resorts in the Adirondacks, where summer homes were springing up in large numbers. In 1922 the company changed its name to the Old Hickory Furniture Company in recognition of their expanded lines. Early goods were identified with the company name burned in on the furniture in inconspicuous spots, while later pieces were given a label or small brass tag. The Old Hickory Furniture Company continued to produce rustic furnishings, especially those popular for outdoor use, well into the 1950s. The plant closed in 1965.

Other Indiana companies noted

and 1940, a wide variety of artistic and bentwood pieces were crafted in this area.

Factory-Made Rustic Furnishings

These were inspired by the early hickory pieces made by unskilled craftsmen in the hill country of the southern states. Among the first and the largest of the hickory furniture manufacturers was the Old Hickory Chair Company of Martinsville, Indiana. The Old Hickory Chair Company christened one of its chairs the Andrew Jackson chair, after Old Hickory himself, and these along with all their other goods were crafted from hickory saplings (which were easy to bend) with bark still in place. All pieces were chemically treated to kill insects and were left with a natural finish or given a coat of varnish.

An Old Hickory Chair Company 1904 catalog offered the Andrew Jack-

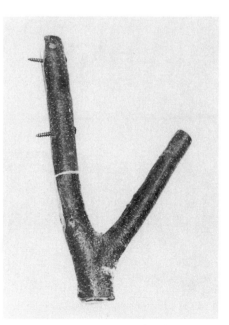

Twig clothing hook, 10″ long, **$3.00.**

Hints on Rustic Twig Furniture

Examine rustic furnishings carefully to make sure they are structurally sound and haven't suffered damage due to dry rot or insects.

Common pieces include planters, chairs, rockers and small tables, while dressers, buffets, desks, beds, gate-leg tables, lamps and serving tables would be rare finds. An Adirondack example of rustic furniture with a mosaic twig design or white bark decoration could be worth several thousand dollars.

Artisans have revived the art of handcrafting rustic furnishings, but their goods are sold as new. However, collectors must be aware that reproduction pieces have been fashioned after Gypsy chairs with a loop-back, but they do not exhibit the patina of aged wood. Check for old nails in joints or for dovetailed joints in case pieces. The popularity of rustic furniture is on the rise and prices are increasing as collectors recognize the cultural importance of these pieces as both a form of folk art and interpretation of beauty and simplicity.

A pair of hickory chairs, painted black, 20″ wide × 32″ tall, **$190 for the pair.**

for their production of hickory furnishings include the Rustic Hickory Furniture Company of Laporte (1902–1933), Indiana Willow Products Company of Martinsville (1937–1956), the Jasper Hickory Furniture Company of Jasper (1928–1938), Indiana Hickory Furniture Company at Colfax (1927–1942), and Columbus Hickory Furniture Company (1930–1950s). Hickory furniture also was produced by inmates at the Indiana State Prison (1929–1960s) and used mainly at state parks.

All of these companies crafted a selection of chairs, rockers, settees, tables, porch swings, planters and benches for outdoor use; some also turned out beds, dressers, washstands, buffets, serving tables, desk, umbrella stands, and lamps for indoor use or to serve on a screened-in porch.

A sampling of prices from the Old Hickory Chair Company catalog of 1912 includes the following: a simple porch chair was $3.50; a rocker $4.25; a settee was $7.50; a round, oak-top porch table cost $8.00; an Andrew Jackson chair was $4.00; a dining room buffet with a beveled plate mirror was $150.00; a ten-foot round extension table was $80.00; a tripod base planter cost $3.00; a single bed was $30.00; a tall writing desk was $60.00; and a child's high chair was $3.00.

A Closing Word

This work has been an endeavor to introduce you to country furniture styles, and to assist you in distinguishing various pieces available on the antiques market today. Information has been presented which will hopefully encourage you to learn more, inspect furniture more closely, and above all, have a greater appreciation of not just nineteenth-century country furniture but also the factory-produced pieces American ingenuity brought us in the early twentieth century.

Bibliography

Books

Andrews, Edward Deming, and Faith Andrews. *Shaker Furniture: The Craftsmanship of an American Communal Sect.* New York: Dover Publications, Inc., 1964. (Unabridged republication of the 1937 work originally published by Yale University Press.)

Blundell, Peter S. *The Marketplace Guide to Oak Furniture Styles and Values.* Paducah, Ky.: Collector Books, 1980.

Comstock, Helen. *American Furniture.* New York: The Viking Press, 1962.

Corbin, Patricia. *All About Wicker.* New York: E.P. Dutton, 1978.

Innes, Miranda. *The Country Home Book.* New York: Simon and Schuster, 1989.

Johansson, Warren I. *Country Furniture and Accessories from Quebec.* West Chester, Pa.: Schiffer Publishing, Ltd., 1990.

Kaye, Myrna. *Fake, Fraud, or Genuine? Identifying Authentic American Antique Furniture.* Boston, Mass.: Little, Brown and Company, 1987.

Kennedy, Philip D. *Hoosier Cabinets.* Philip D. Kennedy, 9256 Holyoke Court, Indianapolis, Ind., 1989.

Ketchum, William C. Jr. *The Catalogue of American Antiques.* New York: Rutledge Books, 1979.

——. *The Knopf Collectors' Guides to American Antiques: Chests, Cupboards, Desks and Other Pieces.* New York: Alfred A. Knopf, 1982.

Kettell, Russell Hawes. *The Pine Furniture of Early New England.* New York: Dover Publications, Inc., replication of 1929 edition.

Kirk, John T. *Early American Furniture.* New York: Alfred A. Knopf, 1970.

——. *The Impecunious Collector's Guide to American Antiques.* New York: Alfred A. Knopf, 1975.

Kovel, Ralph, and Terry Kovel. *American Country Furniture 1780–1875.* New York: Crown Publishers, Inc., 1987.

——. *Know Your Collectibles.* New York: Crown Publishers, Inc., 1981.

Kylloe, Ralph. *The Collected Works of Indiana Hickory Furniture Makers.* Nashua, N.H.: Rustic Publications, 1989.

Lea, Zilla Rider. *The Ornamented Chair: Its Development in America 1700–1890.* Rutland, Vt.: Charles E. Tuttle Company, 1960. (A publication of the Historical Society of Early American Decoration.)

Marsh, Moreton. *The Easy Expert in American Antiques.* New York: J.B. Lippincott Company, 1978.

Michael, George. *Basic Book of Antiques and Collectibles.* Radnor, Pa.: Wallace-Homestead Book Company, 1992.

Miller, Judith, and Martin Miller. *Period Design and Furnishing.* New York: Crown Publishers, Inc., 1989.

Montgomery Ward and Company Spring and Summer 1895 Catalog. New York: Dover Publications, Inc., 1969 publication of unabridged facsimile.

Morykan, Dana N., and Harry L. Rinker. *Warman's Country Antiques and Collectibles.* Radnor, Pa.: Wallace-Homestead Book Company, 1992.

Moulin, Pierre, Pierre LeVec, and Linda Dannenberg. *Pierre Deux's French Country.* New York: Clarkson N. Potter, Inc., 1984.

Mussey, Robert D. Jr. *The First American Furniture Finisher's Manual.* New York: Dover Publications, Inc., 1987. (A reprint of *The Cabinet Makers Guide* of 1827.)

Phillips, Barty. *The Country House Book.* Topsfield, Mass.: Salem House Pubishers, 1988.

Philp, Peter, and Gillian Walking. *Field Guide to Antique Furniture.* Boston,

Mass.: Houghton Mifflin Company, 1992.

Plante, Ellen M. *Kitchen Collectibles: An Illustrated Price Guide.* Radnow, Pa.: Wallace-Homestead Book Company, 1991.

Raycraft, Don, and Carol Raycraft. *American Country Antiques* (twelfth edition). Radnor, Pa.: Wallace-Homestead Book Company, 1992.

Reif, Rita. *The Antique Collector's Guide to Styles and Prices.* New York: Hawthorn Books, Inc., 1970.

Revi, Albert Christian. *The Spinning Wheel's Complete Book of Antiques.* New York: Grosset and Dunlap, 1977.

Rinker, Harry L. *Warman's Americana and Collectibles* (5th edition). Radnor, Pa.: Wallace-Homestead Book Company, 1992.

———. *Warman's Furniture.* Radnor, Pa.: Wallace-Homestead Book Company, 1992.

Schwartz, Marvin D. *The Knopf Collectors' Guides to American Antiques: Chairs, Tables, Sofas and Beds.* New York: Alfred A. Knopf, 1982.

Scott, Tim. *Fine Wicker Furniture 1870–1930.* West Chester, Pa.: Schiffer Publishing, Ltd., 1990.

Shea, John G. *The Pennsylvania Dutch and Their Furniture.* New York: Van Nostrand Reinhold Company, 1980.

Swedberg, Robert W., and Harriett Swedberg. *American Oak Furniture Styles and Prices.* Radnor, Pa.: Wallace-Homestead Book Company, revised edition 1986.

———. *American Oak Furniture Styles and Prices Book II.* Radnor, Pa.: Wallace-Homestead Book Company, 1984.

———. *Country Furniture and Accessories with Prices.* Radnor, Pa.: Wallace-Homestead Book Company, 1983.

———. *Country Furniture and Accessories with Prices Book II.* Radnor, Pa.: Wallace-Homestead Book Company, 1984.

———. *Country Pine Furniture.* Radnor,

Pa.: Wallace-Homestead Book Company, 1983.

Time-Life Books. *American Country Series.* Alexandria, Va.: Time-Life Books Inc., 1988.

Winchester, Alice. *The Antiques Book.* New York: Bonanza Books, 1950.

Articles

Barry, Joan. "Yesterday's Wicker." *Cape Cod Home and Garden* (summer 1991).

Johnson, Bruce E. "Painted Beauties." *Country Living* (November 1991).

Kauffman, Henry J. "Pennsylvania-German Schranks." *The New York-Pennsylvania Collector* (December 1991).

Manroe, Candace Ord. "Roots of Country." *Country Home* (October 1991).

Plante, Ellen M. "In Pursuit of the Hoosier." *Country Living* (April 1988).

———. "Every Woman's Helpmate: The Free-Standing Kitchen Cabinet." *Country Traditional Decorating Ideas* (fall 1990).

———. "Pretty Twisted: The Story of Antique Wireware." *Cape Cod Home and Garden* (winter 1991).

Reed, Robert. "The Wonderful World of Windsor." *Country Traditional* (1991 annual issue).

Rinker, Harry L. "The Evolution of Country." *Country Accents* (September/October 1991).

Saunders, Richard. "American Rustic." *Country Home* (June 1989).

Schiller, Barbara. "As American as . . . a Rocking Chair." *Victorian Homes* (summer 1982).

———. "Wicker." *Victorian Homes* (summer 1983).

———. "Painted Cottage Furniture." *Victorian Homes* (winter 1983).

Wright, Heather. "As the Twig Bends." *Traditional Home* (August 1991).

Index

Page numbers in *italics* refer to illustrations